infused

Susan Elia MacNeal

Photographs by Leigh Beisch

infused

100+ Recipes for Infused Liqueurs and Cocktails

CHRONICLE BOOKS

SAN FRANCISCO

Thank you to Bill LeBlond and
Amy Treadwell of Chronicle Books.

Special thanks, as always,
to Noel MacNeal.

A toast to Idria Barone Knecht.

And cheers to the open-minded
gang of taste-testers: Bob Amini,
Josh Axelrad, James Byrne,
Scott Cameron, Edna MacNeal,
Paul McGuinness, Christine Lloyd,
Lisa Rogers, Danny Vaccaro,
and Kate Wiseman.

Library of Congress Cataloging-in-Publication Data available.

ISBN-10: 0-8118-4600-8
ISBN-13: 978-0-8118-4600-4

Manufactured in China.

Design by Betty Ho and Santiago Giraldo-Tobón
Illustrations and typesetting by Betty Ho

Distributed in Canada by Raincoast Books
9050 Shaughnessy Street
Vancouver, British Columbia V6P 6E5

10 9 8 7 6 5 4 3 2 1

Chronicle Books LLC
85 Second Street
San Francisco, California 94105
www.chroniclebooks.com

Contents

Introduction

Making your own infused liqueurs is simple, and the results are delicious. Creating them is also an act of self-expression, allowing you to play and experiment by inventing and combining flavors. Vodka—clear and neutral tasting—is an ideal blank canvas for infusions. Other spirits work beautifully as well: rum, tequila (especially white or silver tequila), bourbon, brandy, gin, even Cognac if you're feeling especially decadent. Once you've picked your base, the choices of ingredients to infuse are dizzying: fruits, flowers, herbs, spices. The combinations and permutations are endless. The depth of flavor that can be achieved is unparalleled.

In this book, you'll learn not only how to make your own infusions, but also how to mix them to great effect. Lush and aromatic, infused liqueurs intensify the taste of your favorite cocktails—and can inspire you to create new ones. Included here are easy recipes for fashioning an array of liqueurs, as well as cocktail recipes, both classic and creative, for using them. A splash of sweet apricot-infused brandy enlivens Champagne in a Champagne Charlie; other cocktails featuring fizz include the Rose Kiss, with rose petal–infused vodka, and Ernest Hemingway's Corpse Reviver, with anise-infused vodka. Delight in the bergamot-perfumed Earl Grey Martini, the refreshing Tokyo Martini with cucumber-infused vodka and sake, or the cooling Strawberry Meringue, with strawberry vodka and cream. Le Cognac aux Truffles—Cognac infused with truffles—is without comparison. Whether you prefer a tangy cosmopolitan with orange-infused vodka, a classic margarita with lime-infused white tequila, or the tongue-tingling Wasabi Mary with chile-infused vodka, *Infused* will expand and invigorate your repertoire of cocktails. And, should inspiration hit, create your own alchemy by making original liqueurs and signature cocktails.

Mass-produced and overpriced, flavored vodkas have proliferated, and drinks using them have become so widespread (with varying degrees of success) that it's easy to forget that flavored vodkas, as well as brandies, rums, tequilas, and gins, have a long and distinguished history.

The Russians and the Poles were the first to flavor their vodkas, as early as the fifteenth century. Each household would infuse its vodka, called "little water," with various spices and fragrant grasses, as well as different fruits.

The Romanians were known for their plum and prune brandies, while the Hungarians perfected an apricot version. The French flavored their brandies with pears. The Italians used lemons, and the Spanish their local Seville oranges. In Northern Europe, schnapps, cousin of the Russian flavored vodkas, was infused with fruits and spices. The Germans and Swiss savored kirsch, brandy made from cherries. Gin, originally from Holland, is a flavored spirit—a neutral white base distilled from grains flavored with juniper berries, anise, cinnamon, angelica root, orange peel, cassia bark, and coriander.

Although some of these liqueurs are distilled, not infused, the principle is the same—to flavor a base alcohol and produce a liqueur that can be enjoyed on its own or mixed in cocktails.

All infused liqueurs are created using the same basic principle. A flavor is steeped in an alcohol base for a time. The solids are filtered out, and sweetening is added, if desired. The liqueur is aged, which allows the flavors to mellow, then it is bottled and ready to serve. These steps are the simple structure of making a liqueur. It's the details—the specific flavoring, the length of steeping, the particular sweetener—and the variations that give character to the creation.

When making your own infused liqueurs, you're limited only by your imagination and palate. You can use apples, blueberries, peaches, strawberries, or chiles. But what about basil, lychees, rose petals, grilled vegetables, cucumber, or green tea? As a sweetener will you choose white sugar or brown? Exotic honey or maple syrup? And will you use vodka? Or will you try brandy, white tequila, or perhaps dark rum? You decide.

By making your own infused vodkas and liqueurs, and mixing your own drinks, you can help revitalize the art of the cocktail. Experiment with flavor, educate your palate, and enjoy the fruits of your own labor. Share your creations with family and friends.

Infused Liqueurs

Basic Principles of Infusion

Why does the alcohol absorb the flavor of the ingredients? In a word—osmosis. Osmosis is the technical name for the process of water or another solvent passing through a membrane that is fine enough to accommodate the water, but not chemicals with a larger molecular structure.

When you place flavoring agents in alcohol—cherries in brandy, for example—osmosis occurs. At first, the brandy remains outside the cherries, whose skins act as membranes. The water inside each cherry is free to move through the membrane, and once it passes into the brandy, it's likely to stay there. Over time, not only the water but also the sugars, flavors, and colors pass through the skins into the alcohol. The skin and the pits also contribute flavor. When the steeping period is finished, the cherries will be flavorless and have lost most of their color. They can be squeezed into the liqueur and then discarded. Other ingredients will react in a similar manner.

Any alcohol can be infused, but vodka, brandy, rum, and tequila work especially well. Cognac and bourbon are also options. The spirits you use should be good quality, but need not be a top brand. Middle-of-the-road brands are more neutral tasting and will better carry the flavors of the ingredients you're infusing.

However, when it comes to ingredients to infuse, use the absolute premium. In-season fresh fruits and herbs, organically and locally grown, are best. Citrus fruits should be well scrubbed. Flower petals should be organically grown. Use the freshest, best-quality spices and cocoas (replace any in your cupboard that are more than four months old). Splurge on a wonderful honey for sweetening. The difference in flavor is incomparable.

When creating your own infusions, use a glass container. Glass is a nonreactive material that won't taint the flavor. The one thing you should avoid at all costs is air in the container. Oxygen can cause fermentation, wreaking havoc on an infusion, especially one with fruit. So be sure to use an appropriately sized container that keeps oxygen to a minimum. The recommended size in this book's recipes is 2 quarts (2 liters).

In addition to a glass container of the appropriate size, you will need measuring cups and measuring spoons. A vegetable peeler or paring knife is required for some recipes. Consider using a zester to remove citrus zest.

Sweetening is optional for some liqueurs. If you decide to use a sweetener, know that it serves two purposes: it cuts the bitterness, and lowers the alcohol content. If you're using a sweetener with its own unique flavor, such as lavender honey or dark brown sugar, it will add another note of complexity to your liqueur. The amount of sweetening you add depends on many factors—your personal taste, the sweetness of the base alcohol, and the flavoring agents you use. Also consider the purpose of your liqueur. Is it to be drunk straight up or mixed in a particular cocktail? A good rule of thumb is to be conservative when adding sweetener to an infusion. You can always add more, but you can't take any out.

Sugar Syrup
1 cup water
2 cups granulated sugar

Put the water in a small saucepan. Add the sugar. Bring the water to a boil while stirring. Reduce the heat and continue to stir until the sugar dissolves. Cool to room temperature. Select a clean container that will hold at least 1 $\frac{1}{2}$ cups. Using a funnel, pour the sugar syrup into the container, seal, and store in the refrigerator for up to 6 months.

Sweetening Hints
Cool the sugar syrup completely before adding to your infusion, or you will burn off some of the alcohol and affect the flavor.

If your local tap water has a distinctive odor or flavor, use filtered or bottled water for your sugar syrup.

For brown sugar syrup, prepare the recipe as directed using $\frac{3}{4}$ cup brown sugar, $\frac{1}{2}$ cup granulated sugar, and 1 cup water, or substitute 2 cups brown sugar for the granulated sugar.

TO SUBSTITUTE HONEY: $3/4$ unit of honey for each unit of sugar syrup.

TO SUBSTITUTE MAPLE SYRUP: $3/4$ unit of maple syrup for each unit of sugar syrup.

TO SUBSTITUTE MOLASSES: 1 unit of molasses equals $3/4$ unit of granulated sugar (and should replace no more than half the sugar in a recipe).

Brown sugar and honey will slightly change the color of your infusion (adding a light to medium-brown tint); please use accordingly.

Please don't use sugar substitutes.

Adjusting Flavors

If your infusion is too strong, add unflavored vodka (or whatever spirit you're using) to taste.

If your infusion isn't flavorful enough, let it age for another week or two.

If your infusion still isn't flavorful enough (which can happen occasionally with some fruit infusions, particularly the berry variety), strain the infusion and discard the flavorings. Add fresh ingredients and let steep again as directed.

If your infusion is almost but not quite right, try adding another flavor—lemon zest for a fruit infusion in need of complexity, vanilla bean for smoothness, or cinnamon for a little spice.

While many infusions take on semiprecious hues (cherry brandy will turn a lovely dark red, lime vodka a faint green, pumpkin a lovely orange), others will not. Adding natural food coloring (see page 148 for ordering information) is an option. As with sugar, remember that you can always add more, but you can't take any away.

If you're making a combination flavor—chocolate and mint, pink grapefruit and lime, cucumber and rose petal—consider infusing your flavors separately. This allows you to adjust the flavors independently. Once you're satisfied with each, then mix them together.

Apple Liqueur

Decant the spirits into a clean 2-quart (2-liter) glass container with a tight-fitting lid. Soak the original bottle to remove the label. Let dry.

Cut the apples into wedges, leaving the cores and removing the stems. Add to the spirits. Allow the spirits to infuse away from direct sunlight and intense heat for 1 month. Shake the container a few times each week.

When you're satisfied with the intensity of flavor, strain the liqueur through a metal sieve into a bowl. Discard the apples. Add the sugar syrup to taste, if desired.

Using a funnel, pour the liqueur into the original bottle (or another container). Label with the name of the liqueur and the date. Age the liqueur for 1 month away from light and heat.

VARIATION: Try brown sugar syrup (page 11) or your favorite honey as a sweetener.

750-ml **bottle of brandy, vodka, rum, or Cognac**

10 **apples, such as Granny Smith, Macintosh, and/or Red Delicious, washed thoroughly**

1/4 to 1 **cup sugar syrup (page 11; optional)**

Spiced Apple Pie Liqueur
Add 2 cinnamon sticks, 10 whole cloves, and 1 vanilla bean, split lengthwise, with the apples.

Apricot Liqueur

750-ml bottle of brandy, vodka, rum, or Cognac

15 to 18 apricots, washed thoroughly

1/4 to 1 cup sugar syrup (page 11; optional)

Decant the spirits into a clean 2-quart (2-liter) glass container with a tight-fitting lid. Soak the original bottle to remove the label. Let dry.

Cut the apricots in half and thinly slice. Add the apricots and their pits to the spirits. Allow the spirits to infuse away from direct sunlight and intense heat for 1 month. Shake the container a few times each week.

When you're satisfied with the intensity of flavor, strain the liqueur through a metal sieve into a bowl. Discard the apricots and pits. Add the sugar syrup to taste, if desired.

Using a funnel, pour the liqueur into the original bottle (or another container). Label with the name of the liqueur and the date. Age the liqueur for 1 month away from light and heat.

Berry Liqueur

Decant the spirits into a clean 2-quart (2-liter) glass container with a tight-fitting lid. Soak the original bottle to remove the label. Let dry.

If using frozen berries, allow them to thaw. Place the fresh or thawed frozen berries in a bowl, crush with a fork, and add to the spirits. Allow the spirits to infuse away from direct sunlight and intense heat for 3 months. Shake the container a few times each week.

When you're satisfied with the intensity of flavor, strain the liqueur through a metal sieve into a bowl. Discard the berries. Add the sugar syrup to taste, if desired.

Using a funnel, pour the liqueur into the original bottle (or another container). Label with the name of the liqueur and the date. Age for 1 month away from light and heat.

VARIATIONS: Add the zest of $1/2$ lemon, 3 or 4 whole cloves, $1/2$ cinnamon stick, and/or $1/2$ vanilla bean, split lengthwise, with the berries.

Substitute $1/4$ to 1 cup honey for the sugar syrup.

750-ml bottle of brandy, vodka, rum, or tequila

1 quart fresh berries, such as black currants, blueberries, cherries, raspberries, strawberries, and/or cranberries, or one 16-ounce package frozen berries

$1/4$ to 1 cup sugar syrup (page 11; optional)

Red Chile Liqueur

750-ml **bottle of vodka or tequila**

1 **red serrano or habanero chile**

3 **red jalapeño chiles**

Decant the spirits into a clean 2-quart (2-liter) glass container with a tight-fitting lid. Soak the original bottle to remove the label. Let dry.

Wearing rubber gloves to protect against irritating oils, cut each chile in half lengthwise. Remove and discard the stems, seeds, and ribs. Add the chiles to the spirits. Allow the spirits to infuse away from direct sunlight and intense heat for 2 days. Shake the container a few times each day.

When you're satisfied with the intensity of flavor, strain the liqueur through a metal sieve into a bowl. Discard the chiles.

Using a funnel, pour the liqueur into the original bottle (or another container). Label with the name of the liqueur and the date. Age the liqueur for 2 weeks away from light and heat.

Green Chile Liqueur

Substitute 1 green chile for the 1 red serrano or habanero chile.

Thai Chile Liqueur

Substitute 3 Thai chiles for the 1 red serrano or habanero chile.

Chocolate Liqueur

Decant the spirits into a clean 2-quart (2-liter) glass container with a tight-fitting lid. Soak the original bottle to remove the label. Let dry.

Add the cocoa powder to the spirits and stir to combine. Allow the spirits to infuse away from direct sunlight and intense heat for at least 2 weeks or up to 1 month. Shake the container a few times each week.

When you're satisfied with the intensity of flavor, strain the liqueur through a coffee filter into a bowl. Discard any solids. Strain again if necessary. Add the sugar syrup to taste.

Using a funnel, pour the liqueur into the original bottle (or another container). Label with the name of the liqueur and the date. Age the liqueur for 1 month away from heat and light.

VARIATIONS: Add 1 vanilla bean, split lengthwise, or 1 teaspoon vanilla extract, the zest of $1/2$ orange, or 1 cinnamon stick with the cocoa powder.

750-ml bottle of brandy, vodka, or Cognac

1 cup best-quality unsweetened cocoa powder

2 to 3 cups sugar syrup (page 11)

White Chocolate Liqueur

Substitute 1 cup best-quality unsweetened white chocolate powder for the cocoa powder.

Grapefruit Liqueur

750-ml bottle of brandy, vodka, rum, tequila, gin, or Cognac

4 medium-sized yellow, pink, or red grapefruits, scrubbed thoroughly

¹⁄₄ to 1 cup sugar syrup (page 11; optional)

Decant the spirits into a clean 2-quart (2-liter) glass container with a tight-fitting lid. Soak the original bottle to remove the label. Let dry.

Using a vegetable peeler, paring knife, or zester, remove the zest from each citrus fruit in strips, avoiding any of the white pith. Reserve the flesh for another use. Add the zest strips to the spirits. Allow the spirits to infuse away from direct sunlight and intense heat for 2 to 3 weeks. Shake the container a few times each week.

When you're satisfied with the intensity of flavor, strain the liqueur through a metal sieve into a bowl. Discard the zest. Add the sugar syrup to taste, if desired.

Using a funnel, pour the liqueur into the original bottle (or another container). Label with the name of the liqueur and the date. Age the liqueur for 1 month away from light and heat.

Lemon Liqueur

Substitute 8 lemons, scrubbed thoroughly, for the grapefruits.

Lime Liqueur

Substitute 12 limes, scrubbed thoroughly, for the grapefruits.

Orange Liqueur

Substitute 6 oranges, scrubbed thoroughly, for the grapefruits.

Tangerine Liqueur

Substitute 10 tangerines, scrubbed thoroughly, for the grapefruits.

Coffee Liqueur

Decant the spirits into a clean 2-quart (2-liter) glass container with a tight-fitting lid. Soak the original bottle to remove the label. Let dry.

Add the instant coffee powder to the spirits and stir to combine. Allow the spirits to infuse away from direct sunlight or intense heat for 1 month. Shake the container a few times each week.

When you're satisfied with the intensity of flavor, strain the liqueur through a coffee filter into a bowl. Discard any solids. Add the sugar syrup to taste.

Using a funnel, pour the liqueur into the original bottle (or another container). Label with the name of the liqueur and the date. Age for 1 month away from light and heat.

VARIATIONS: Sugar syrup made from light or dark brown sugar (page 11) complements the coffee flavor. Add 1 vanilla bean, split lengthwise, or 2 teaspoons vanilla extract with the coffee powder to smooth out the flavor.

750-ml bottle of brandy, vodka, rum, tequila, or Cognac

1 cup instant coffee powder

2 to 3 cups sugar syrup (page 11)

Cucumber Liqueur

750-ml **bottle of vodka, gin, or tequila**

2 **cups peeled, sliced cucumber**

1/4 to 1 **cup sugar syrup (page 11; optional)**

Decant the spirits into a clean 2-quart (2-liter) glass container with a tight-fitting lid. Soak the original bottle to remove the label. Let dry.

Add the cucumber slices to the spirits. Allow the spirits to infuse away from direct sunlight and intense heat for 1 month. Shake the container a few times each week.

When you're satisfied with the intensity of flavor, strain the liqueur through a metal sieve into a bowl. Discard the cucumber slices. Add the sugar syrup to taste, if desired.

Using a funnel, pour the liqueur into the original bottle (or another container). Label with the name of the liqueur and the date. Age the liqueur for 1 month away from light and heat.

Fennel Liqueur

Substitute 2 cups sliced fennel bulb for the cucumber.

Rhubarb Liqueur

Substitute 2 cups sliced rhubarb for the cucumber.

Elderflower Liqueur

Decant the spirits into a clean 2-quart (2-liter) glass container with a tight-fitting lid. Soak the original bottle to remove the label. Let dry.

Add the petals to the spirits. Allow the spirits to infuse away from direct sunlight and intense heat for 2 to 3 weeks. Shake the container a few times each week.

When you're satisfied with the intensity of flavor, strain the liqueur through a metal sieve into a bowl. Discard the petals. Add the sugar syrup to taste, if desired.

Using a funnel, pour the liqueur into the original bottle (or another container). Label with the name of the liqueur and the date. Age the liqueur for 1 month away from light and heat.

VARIATION: Use your favorite honey as a sweetener in place of the sugar syrup.

750-ml bottle of vodka or gin

2 cups lightly packed organically grown elderflower petals, rinsed and patted dry

1/4 to 1 cup sugar syrup (page 11; optional)

Lavender Liqueur

Substitute 3 tablespoons organically grown lavender buds, dried or fresh, for the elderflower petals.

Rose Liqueur

Substitute 2 cups lightly packed, organically grown rose petals for the elder-flower petals.

Violet Liqueur

Substitute 2 cups lightly packed, stemmed, organically grown violets for the elder-flower petals.

Gazpacho Liqueur

750-ml bottle of vodka or tequila

3 large poblano chiles

1 red bell pepper, cut into quarters

4 tomatoes, halved

1 large Vidalia onion, cut into 1-inch-thick slices

1 cucumber, peeled and halved lengthwise

2 celery stalks, trimmed

1 clove garlic, halved

Preheat the broiler.

Decant the spirits into a clean 2-quart (2-liter) glass container with a tight-fitting lid. Soak the original bottle to remove the label. Let dry.

Wearing rubber gloves to protect against irritating oils, cut each chile in half lengthwise. Remove the stems, seeds, and ribs. Remove the stem from the bell pepper. Cut lengthwise into quarters and remove the seeds and ribs.

Arrange the chiles, bell pepper, tomatoes, onion, cucumber, celery, and garlic on a baking sheet. Grill, turning as needed, until blistered and blackened in places, about 20 minutes. Remove the baking sheet from the broiler and let the vegetables cool.

Slice the grilled vegetables and add all of them to the spirits. Allow the spirits to infuse away from direct sunlight and intense heat for 1 month. Shake the container a few times each week.

When you're satisfied with the intensity of flavor, strain the liqueur through a metal sieve into a bowl. Discard the solids. Strain again through a coffee filter, if necessary.

Using a funnel, pour the liqueur into the original bottle (or another container). Label with the name of the liqueur and the date. Age the liqueur for 1 month away from light and heat.

Onion Liqueur

Substitute 2 large Vidalia onions, coarsely chopped, for the vegetables.

Basil Liqueur

Decant the spirits into a clean 2-quart (2-liter) glass container with a tight-fitting lid. Soak the original bottle to remove the label. Let dry.

Add the basil to the spirits. Allow the spirits to infuse away from direct sunlight and intense heat for 24 hours.

When you're satisfied with the intensity of flavor, strain the liqueur through a coffee filter. Discard the basil.

Using a funnel, pour the liqueur into the original bottle (or another container). Label with the name of the liqueur and the date. Age the liqueur for 1 week away from light and heat.

VARIATIONS: Substitute 1 cup lightly packed tarragon, thyme, or sage leaves, preferably organic, rinsed and patted dry, for the basil.

750-ml bottle of vodka or tequila

1 cup lightly packed basil leaves, preferably organic, rinsed and patted dry

Mint Liqueur

Substitute 1 cup lightly packed spearmint or peppermint leaves, preferably organic, rinsed and patted dry, for the basil. You may substitute bourbon for the vodka or tequila and add 1/4 to 1 cup sugar syrup (page 11).

Rosemary Liqueur

Substitute 1 cup rosemary, preferably organic, rinsed and patted dry, for the basil.

Lychee Liqueur

750-ml **bottle of vodka or gin**

3 **cups fresh lychees, peeled and pitted**

1/4 to 1 **cup sugar syrup (page 11; optional)**

Decant the spirits into a clean 2-quart (2-liter) glass container with a tight-fitting lid. Soak the original bottle to remove the label. Let dry.

Add the lychees to the spirits. Allow the spirits to infuse away from direct sunlight and intense heat for 2 to 3 weeks. Shake the container a few times each week.

When you're satisfied with the intensity of flavor, strain the liqueur through a metal sieve into a bowl. Discard the lychees. Add the sugar syrup to taste, if desired.

Using a funnel, pour the liqueur into the original bottle (or another container). Label with the name of the liqueur and the date. Age the liqueur for 1 month away from heat and light.

Mango Liqueur

Decant the spirits into a clean 2-quart (2-liter) glass container with a tight-fitting lid. Soak the original bottle to remove the label. Let dry.

Add the mango slices to the spirits. Allow the spirits to infuse away from direct sunlight and intense heat for 1 month. Shake the container a few times each week.

When you're satisfied with the intensity of flavor, strain the liqueur through a metal sieve into a bowl. Discard the mango. Add the sugar syrup to taste, if desired.

Using a funnel, pour the liqueur into the original bottle (or another container). Label with the name of the liqueur and the date. Age the liqueur for 1 month away from light and heat.

750-ml bottle of brandy, vodka, rum, tequila, or Cognac

3 cups sliced mango

1/4 to 1 cup sugar syrup (page 11; optional)

NOTE: Mangoes can sometimes be difficult to infuse. If the flavor does not fully infuse the vodka, add 2 to 3 teaspoons of melon syrup, the kind used at coffeehouses (see page 148 for ordering information), or to taste.

Peach Liqueur

750-ml	**bottle of brandy, vodka, rum, tequila, or Cognac**
12	**peaches**
1/4 to 1	**cup sugar syrup (page 11; optional)**

Decant the spirits into a clean 2-quart (2-liter) glass container with a tight-fitting lid. Soak the original bottle to remove the label. Let dry.

Cut the peaches in half and thinly slice. Add the peaches and their pits to the spirits. Allow the spirits to infuse away from direct sunlight and intense heat for 1 month. Shake the container a few times each week.

When you're satisfied with the intensity of flavor, strain the liqueur through a metal sieve into a bowl. Discard the solids. Add the sugar syrup to taste, if desired.

Using a funnel, pour the liqueur into the original bottle (or another container). Label with the name of the liqueur and the date. Age the liqueur for 1 month away from light and heat.

VARIATIONS: Use your favorite honey in place of the sugar syrup. Add 1 vanilla bean, split lengthwise, the zest of $1/2$ lemon, or 6 whole cloves with the peaches.

Pear Liqueur

Decant the spirits into a clean 2-quart (2-liter) glass container with a tight-fitting lid. Soak the original bottle to remove the label. Let dry.

Slice the pears, keeping the cores intact. Add the pears to the spirits. Allow the spirits to infuse away from direct sunlight and intense heat for 1 month. Shake the container a few times each week.

When you're satisfied with the intensity of flavor, strain the liqueur through a metal sieve into a bowl. Discard the pears. Add the sugar syrup to taste, if desired.

Using a funnel, pour the liqueur into the original bottle (or another container). Label with the name of the liqueur and the date. Age the liqueur for 1 month away from light and heat.

VARIATIONS: Use honey in place of the sugar syrup. Add 2 cinnamon sticks and/or 6 whole cloves with the pears.

750-ml bottle of brandy, vodka, rum, tequila, or Cognac

6 large pears, preferably Bartlett

1/4 to 1 cup sugar syrup (page 11; optional)

Peppercorn Liqueur

750-ml **bottle of vodka or tequila**

¹/₂ **cup black, pink, and/or white peppercorns**

Decant the spirits into a clean 2-quart (2-liter) glass container with a tight-fitting lid. Soak the original bottle to remove the label. Let dry.

Using a mortar and pestle, crush the peppercorns slightly. Add to the spirits. Allow the spirits to infuse away from direct sunlight and intense heat for 2 to 4 weeks. Shake the container a few times each week.

When you're satisfied with the intensity of flavor, strain the liqueur through a coffee filter. Discard the peppercorns.

Using a funnel, pour the liqueur into the original bottle (or another container). Label with the name of the liqueur and the date. Age the liqueur for 1 month away from light and heat.

Pumpkin Liqueur

Decant the spirits into a clean 2-quart (2-liter) glass container with a tight-fitting lid. Soak the original bottle to remove the label. Let dry.

Add the pumpkin and spices to the spirits. Allow the spirits to infuse away from direct sunlight and intense heat for 1 month. Shake the container a few times each week.

When you're satisfied with the intensity of flavor, strain the liqueur through a metal sieve into a bowl. Discard the solids. Strain the liqueur again through a coffee filter, if necessary. Add the sugar syrup to taste, if desired.

Using a funnel, pour the liqueur into the original bottle (or another container). Label with the name of the liqueur and the date. Age the liqueur for 1 month away from light and heat.

750-ml bottle of brandy, vodka, rum, tequila, or Cognac

1 cup canned pumpkin

1 vanilla bean, split lengthwise, or 2 teaspoons vanilla extract

2 cinnamon sticks

20 whole cloves

One 2-inch piece of fresh ginger, peeled and cut into 1/4-inch-thick slices

1/4 to 1 cup sugar syrup (page 11; optional)

Anise Liqueur

750-ml bottle of brandy, vodka, rum, tequila, or Cognac

2 tablespoons anise seeds

1/4 to 1 cup sugar syrup (page 11; optional)

Decant the spirits into a clean 2-quart (2-liter) glass container with a tight-fitting lid. Soak the original bottle to remove the label. Let dry.

Using a mortar and pestle, crack the anise seeds to release their fragrance. Add the seeds to the spirits. Allow the spirits to infuse away from direct light and intense heat for 1 week. Shake the container a few times each day.

When you're satisfied with the intensity of flavor, strain the liqueur through a coffee filter into a bowl. Discard the seeds. Add the sugar syrup to taste, if desired.

Using a funnel, pour the liqueur into the original bottle (or another container). Label with the name of the liqueur and the date. Age the liqueur for 1 month away from light and heat.

VARIATION: Replace the sugar syrup with honey.

Cinnamon Liqueur

Substitute 4 cinnamon sticks, broken into pieces, for the anise seeds

Spiced Liqueur

Substitute 1 vanilla bean, split lengthwise, 5 whole nutmegs, lightly cracked, 5 cinnamon sticks, broken into pieces, and 10 whole cloves, lightly cracked, for the anise seeds.

Ginger Liqueur

Substitute 2 pieces of fresh ginger, about 4 ounces total, peeled and chopped, for the anise seeds. Add more sugar syrup, up to 2 cups. Infuse for 1 month instead of 1 week. The intensity of fresh ginger varies; you may need more or less depending on your taste. You can also use 1 cup Japanese pickled ginger in place of fresh ginger.

Tea Liqueur

Decant the spirits into a clean 2-quart (2-liter) glass container with a tight-fitting lid. Soak the original bottle to remove the label. Let dry.

Add the tea leaves to the spirits. Allow the spirits to infuse away from direct sunlight and intense heat for no more than 24 hours (any longer will cause the infusion to become bitter).

Strain the liqueur through a metal sieve into a bowl. Discard the tea leaves. Add the sugar syrup to taste, if desired.

Using a funnel, pour the liqueur into the original bottle (or another container). Label with the name of the liqueur and the date. Age the liqueur for 2 weeks away from light and heat.

750-ml bottle of vodka, rum, or gin

1/4 cup best-quality loose tea leaves, such as **Earl Grey, Darjeeling, green, jasmine, rose petal,** or **rose hip**

1/4 to 1 cup sugar syrup (page 11; optional)

Toasted Nut Liqueur

1 cup	sliced almonds or roughly chopped walnuts or hazelnuts or 2 cups shredded coconut
750-ml	bottle of brandy, vodka, rum, tequila, or Cognac
1/4 to 1 cup	sugar syrup (page 11; optional)

Preheat the oven to 350°F. Spread the nuts (or coconut) on a baking sheet and bake until lightly toasted, about 5 minutes. Alternatively, place the nuts in a heavy saucepan over medium-high heat and toast, tossing frequently.

Decant the spirits into a clean 2-quart (2-liter) glass container with a tight-fitting lid. Soak the original bottle to remove the label. Let dry.

Add the nuts to the spirits. Allow the spirits to infuse away from direct sunlight and intense heat for at least 2 weeks or up to 1 month. Shake the container a few times each week.

When you're satisfied with the intensity of flavor, strain the liqueur through a metal strainer into a bowl. Discard the nuts. Add the sugar syrup to taste, if desired.

Using a funnel, pour the liqueur into the original bottle (or another container). Label with the name of the liqueur and the date. Age the liqueur for 1 month away from light and heat.

VARIATIONS: Add 1 vanilla bean, split lengthwise, 1 teaspoon orange zest, 1 teaspoon lemon zest, 1 cinnamon stick, broken into pieces, or 3 whole cloves for additional flavoring.

If you use a sweetener, try brown sugar syrup or honey in place of the sugar syrup.

Truffle Liqueur

AS MADE FROM FRANCE'S RENOWNED EDIBLE FUNGUS BY THE BAR CAMBON AT THE RITZ PARIS AND REPRINTED WITH GRACIOUS PERMISSION.

Decant the Cognac into a clean 2-quart (2-liter) glass container with a tight-fitting lid. Soak the original bottle to remove the label. Let dry.

Add the diced truffle to the Cognac. Allow the Cognac to infuse away from direct sunlight and intense heat for 1 month. Shake the container a few times each week.

When you're satisfied with the intensity of flavor, strain the liqueur through a metal sieve into a bowl and discard the truffle.

Using a funnel, pour the liqueur into the original bottle (or another container). Label with the name of the liqueur and the date. Age for 1 month away from light and heat.

750-ml bottle of best-quality Cognac, such as Hennessy X.O Cognac

1 1/2 ounces truffle, diced

Vanilla Liqueur

750-ml **bottle of brandy, vodka, bourbon, rum, or Cognac**

2 **vanilla beans, split lengthwise**

1/4 to 1 **cup sugar syrup (page 11; optional)**

Decant the spirits into a clean 2-quart (2-liter) glass container with a tight-fitting lid. Soak the original bottle to remove the label. Let dry.

Add the split vanilla beans, including the seeds, to the spirits. Allow the spirits to infuse away from direct sunlight and intense heat for 1 month. Shake the container a few times each week.

When you're satisfied with the intensity of flavor, strain the liqueur through a coffee filter into a bowl. Discard the solids. Strain again if necessary. Add the sugar syrup to taste, if desired.

Using a funnel, pour the liqueur into the original bottle (or another container). Label with the name of the liqueur and the date. Age the liqueur for 1 month away from light and heat.

Watermelon Liqueur

Decant the spirits into a clean 2-quart (2-liter) glass container with a tight-fitting lid. Soak the original bottle to remove the label. Let dry.

Add the watermelon to the spirits. Allow the spirits to infuse away from direct sunlight and intense heat for at least 2 weeks or up to 1 month. Shake the container a few times each week.

When you're satisfied with the intensity of flavor, strain the liqueur through a metal sieve into a bowl. Discard the watermelon. Add the sugar syrup to taste, if desired.

Using a funnel, pour the liqueur into the original bottle (or another container). Label with the name of the liqueur and the date. Age the liqueur for 1 month away from light and heat.

750-ml bottle of vodka, rum, or tequila

3 cups cubed watermelon

1/4 to 1 cup sugar syrup (page 11; optional)

Cocktails

& How to Mix Them

History of the Cocktail

The first reference to before-dinner drinks was recorded in 37 C.E., during the reign of Emperor Tiberius. Pliny the Elder noted in his writings that "it was established that people might drink on an empty stomach and wine-drinking could come before meals."

It took a little while longer for the actual cocktail to appear. Its exact origin is shrouded in mystery, although, appropriately enough for this book, the first one is thought to have been infused. A drink called "cock's ale" was served in early colonial times during cock-fights. A sack containing a parboiled chicken, raisins, mace, and brown sugar was placed in the ale and left to ferment for approximately nine days.

According to some sources, "cocktail" could have been the name of the mixed dregs served up in British taverns—*cock* being the word for "valve" and *tale* referring to the bottom of the spirit barrels. Others recount that during Revolutionary War times, New York tavern keeper Betsey Flanagan supposedly stuck a rooster feather in her glass one day while her French customers shouted "Vive le cocktail!" The term may have come from the old French word *coquetel*, a kind of mixed drink, or perhaps from *kaketal*, the West African word for "scorpion." A letter to the Hudson New York Balance and Columbian Repository in 1806 defined a cocktail as "a stimulating liqueur, composed of spirits of any kind, sugar, water, and bitters."

By the end of the mid-1800s, plenty of cocktails, such as Manhattans (attributed by some to Jenny Churchill, Winston Churchill's mother) and daiquiris, were being mixed and served. The first cocktail book, *The Bartender's Guide: The Bon-Vivant's Companion*, was written in 1862 by bartender Jerry Thomas. It contained "Clear and Reliable Directions for Mixing all the Beverages Used in the United States, Together with The Most Popular British, French, German, Italian, Russian and Spanish Recipes, Embracing Punches, Juleps, Cobblers, etc In Endless Variety." While different cocktails have gone in and out of style over the ages—absinthe frappés in the early twentieth century, martinis during Prohibition, rum and Cokes during World War II, piña coladas in the 1950s, margaritas in the 1970s—some have endured.

The 1990s ushered in a new wave of martini popularity; however, most of these drinks bear no resemblance to the classic (gin, vermouth, a splash of orange bitters, and a lemon twist) except for the glass (a cocktail glass, although often erroneously referred to as a martini glass). The *Sex and the City* girls made famous the so-called cosmo, also known as the cosmopolitan, as well as other drinks in cocktail glasses that could be matched to one's ensemble. While cocktail snobs derided the new martinis based on flavored vodkas, these hybrids seem to be here to stay. The problem with these "juice boxes for yuppies" or "chick drinks," as they're also called, isn't that they are sweet, or contain fruit juices, but that they're often made using overly sweet mixers containing corn syrup, sodium, and artificial flavors and colors. A cosmo prepared from cranberry and orange vodkas and freshly squeezed lime juice is a universe away from its cousin based on premixed syrup.

Most of the drinks in this book are made using already sweetened liqueur, but if you want to add sweetness, it's best to use bar sugar. Also known as superfine or castor sugar, it dissolves quickly and easily, and won't leave a gritty residue at the bottom of a glass. You can also make a simple sugar syrup (page 11) and use it spoon for spoon in recipes calling for sugar.

Equipment
Many drink-making accoutrements are available, but a good stainless-steel shaker is the basic piece you will need. The shaker serves to combine the ingredients for a drink and, when ice is added, to chill them. It consists of three parts: a metal tumbler, a snug-fitting lid, and a small cap that fits over the lid and covers the strainer built into the lid.

A Hawthorne strainer, with a wire spring around the rim, keeps the ice in the shaker and lets you pour more quickly, but isn't necessary if you're making only a drink or two at a time. If you're making a single or double, the strainer that comes with your shaker is adequate.

For measuring alcohols for a crowd, a jigger is essential. The standard two-sider has a measure of 1 1/4 fluid ounces in one bowl and 3/4 fluid ounce in the other. If you do not have a jigger, keep in mind that 2 tablespoons equal 1 fluid ounce.

A manual juicer is inexpensive and works just fine for cocktails made in small quantities. If you are making drinks that use fresh juice in larger quantities, you may want to consider purchasing an electric juicer, if you don't already have one. There are many models available in a wide price range.

A blender is useful for mixed frozen drinks, such as piña coladas. Blenders come in a wide price range. For the purposes of cocktail making, a simple blender is more than adequate.

A zester is useful for making professional-looking lemon and lime twists.

A long-handled bar spoon has many uses, including mixing drinks that aren't shaken and extracting the last olives from the bottom of a jar.

Many bars are quite persnickety about which cocktail should be served in which glass. This is not essential for enjoying mixed drinks. A small selection will do. The most typically used bar glasses are:

Collins glass—tall, thin glass, perfect for highballs (drinks that contain alcohol, ice, and soda) such as gin and tonics or Cuba libres.

Old-fashioned glass—short, squat glass for drinking classic drinks, such as Bloody Marys, mint juleps, and White Russians, served on the rocks. Real old-fashioned glasses have a slightly concave bottom, which is better for muddling (bruising an herb or fruit to release its essence). Also called rocks glass.

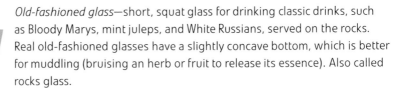

Cocktail glass—shallow bowl with a long stem, often referred to as a martini glass. It's for drinks served straight up (without ice), instead of on the rocks (over ice). Holding the glass by the long stem, instead of the bowl, ensures that the drink will stay cold longer.

Champagne flute—tall, thin glass with a stem that helps drinks with sparkling wine or French Champagne keep their bubbles longer. Holding the tall, thin stem helps keep drinks cold.

Bordeaux glass—oversized glass with a tall bowl and a narrow rim that causes the drink to flow directly to the parts of the tongue that sense fruity and sour tastes. It is for wine-based drinks or exotic drinks with fruit juices.

The glasses you use should be chilled. Fill the glass with ice before you mix the drink and then empty it when you're ready to pour. Better yet, keep your glasses in the freezer. You can frost glasses by dipping them into water and placing them in the freezer while still dripping wet. Leave them for two to three hours.

Ingredients

The point of a good cocktail is to celebrate flavors, not mask them. Therefore, buy the best-quality alcohol you can.

Premade mixers and sweetened juices are full of corn syrup, sodium, and artificial colors and flavors. Would you ever drink this stuff straight, not mixed with alcohol? Probably not. Then spare your drinks. Fresh fruit juice—instead of, say, sour mix—will elevate your drinks to another plane entirely.

Finishing Touches

The purpose of the twist is to add a few drops of citrus oil to the drink. **TO MAKE A TWIST:** Cut a 1-inch-long and $1/8$-inch-wide strip of zest from a well-scrubbed lemon (or other citrus fruit) with a zester or paring knife. Be sure that the zest doesn't include any pith (the white part), as it can make the drink bitter. Hold the zest strip over the drink, and twist it slightly to release the oils. Mixologists debate whether or not to include the twist in the drink, but it looks pretty, and that's always a plus.

To coat the rim of a glass, rub the rim with a small wedge of lemon or lime, then dip it in a saucer of superfine sugar (if you're making a sidecar, say) or coarse salt (for a margarita or paloma).

Ice needs to be freshly made (this way there's no danger of freezer taste), from filtered or spring water, if possible. For mixing drinks in a shaker, you need cracked ice—not ice cubes. If you don't have a block of ice and an ice pick—or if your freezer doesn't crush ice automatically—you'll need a plastic bag and a mallet. Place the ice in the bag and use the mallet to crush it.

Cracked ice is used because it has more surface area than cubes and will therefore chill drinks quickly. If you're using ice in drinks to keep them cold (on the rocks), you'll want ice cubes, which have less surface area, and therefore melt more slowly.

Garnishes can be extremely simple—a strip of lemon zest or a slice of orange—or they can be exotic and unusual—a fresh rose petal or a candied violet. Fresh ingredients are always good—berries, fruits, herbs, and edible flowers, as well as spices and olives—and can all transform a simple cocktail.

Tips for Making Cocktails

Before you mix your infusion into a cocktail, sample it on its own—straight up, on the rocks, or with club soda. You'll be able to appreciate the flavor and understand how it will mix with other ingredients.

Always add the least expensive ingredient (juice, vermouth, whatever) first. That way, if you use too much, you can always pour a little out.

Shaking chills a drink, blends it, dilutes it (ever so slightly, which improves the flavor), and leaves it with lovely flecks of ice. However, it does make a drink just the slightest bit cloudy. If clarity is important, then by all means stir. A good rule of thumb is to shake drinks like martinis, which are all or mostly alcohol, and to stir drinks like the Cuba libre, which are mostly juice or soda. And never shake a drink that contains sparkling wine! You'll lose precious bubbles. How long to shake or stir? As a general rule, shake for 10 to 15 seconds and stir for 20 to 30 seconds. Any longer will provide additional dilution, but won't make your drink any colder.

Drinks, like many things these days, have become supersized. Compare the elegant little coupes that Nick and Nora Charles constantly refilled in *The Thin Man* with today's gargantuan cocktail glasses. It's far better to serve two, small, perfectly chilled drinks to a guest than an enormous one that will become warm and lose flavor.

Attribution of Cocktails

Many bartenders are artists, but instead of a signed painting, they leave behind a recipe, one that's often changed and passed on over the years. Whenever possible, I've tried to refer to the original creator of the drinks listed. There's romance in a cocktail history. Whether a drink is from Bar Hemingway at the Ritz Paris in the 1920s, Harry's Bar in Venice in the 1930s, Gramercy Tavern in New York this past year, or the local pub across the street, part of the enjoyment of sipping a cocktail is in knowing and appreciating its origin and history.

New & Classic Cocktails

Apple Martini

Tangy and fresh, this infused version is a world away from those neon-green apple martinis using store-bought, artificially flavored and colored apple liqueur.

1 **ounce Apple Vodka or Apple Brandy (page 13)**

1 **ounce plain vodka**

1 **ounce apple juice, preferably organic**

1 **cup cracked ice**

1 **thin slice of green apple**

Combine the vodkas, apple juice, and cracked ice in a shaker. Shake for 10 to 15 seconds, then strain into a chilled cocktail glass. Garnish with the green apple slice.

Apple Pie Martini

Full of apple flavor, but also perfumed with vanilla
and spices. Substituting half-and-half or heavy cream
for the apple juice or cider creates an equally luscious
drink.

Serves 1

- **1 ounce fresh-pressed nonalcoholic apple cider**
- **1 ounce Vanilla Vodka (page 34)**
- **1 ounce Apple Vodka or Apple Brandy (page 13)**
- **Splash of Spiced Vodka (page 30)**
- **1 cup cracked ice**
- **1 cinnamon stick**

Combine the apple cider, vodkas, and cracked ice in
a shaker. Shake for 10 to 15 seconds, then strain into a
chilled cocktail glass. Garnish with the cinnamon stick.

Basil Martini

Serves 1

Basil-infused vodka adds an aromatic, mildly pep-
pery, almost minty flavor to a cocktail inspired by Nick
Mautone's version at the Gramercy Tavern in New
York City.

> 3 ounces Basil Vodka (page 23)
>
> 1/2 ounce dry vermouth
>
> 1 cup cracked ice
>
> A few fresh basil leaves

Combine the vodka, vermouth, and cracked ice in a shaker.
Shake for 10 to 15 seconds, then strain into a chilled cocktail glass. Garnish with the basil leaves.

Black Pepper Bloody Mary

The Bloody Mary was created by Fernand "the Frog" Petiot in 1921 at Harry's New York Bar in Paris. Ernest Hemingway, one of the bar's regulars, became the drink's champion and spread the formula throughout the world. The following recipe contains the classic Bloody Mary ingredients—tomato and lemon juices and Tabasco sauce—plus Black Peppercorn Vodka to add even more stinging heat.

Serves 1

4 or 5	ice cubes
2	ounces Black Peppercorn Vodka (page 28)
1/2	cup tomato juice
1 1/2	teaspoons fresh lemon juice
	Splash of Worcestershire sauce
3 or 4	dashes of Tabasco sauce
1	cup cracked ice
	Pinch of salt
	Pinch of freshly ground pepper
1	celery stick
1	lemon wedge

Place the ice cubes in a chilled collins glass. Combine the vodka, tomato and lemon juices, Worcestershire and Tabasco sauces, and cracked ice in a shaker. Shake for 10 to 15 seconds, then strain over the ice cubes. Season with the salt and pepper and garnish with the celery stick and lemon wedge.

Blueberry Crush

A glorious cocktail with a gorgeous deep purple hue that evokes the warm twilight of midsummer evenings.

4 or 5   ice cubes

    2   blackberries

    2   blueberries

    2   raspberries

    3   ounces Blueberry Vodka (page 15)

         Dash of lime juice

    1   cup cracked ice

  1/2   cup sparkling water or club soda (optional)

Place the ice cubes in a chilled old-fashioned glass. Place the berries in a small bowl and crush with a fork. Add to a shaker with the vodka, lime juice, and cracked ice. Shake for 10 to 15 seconds, then strain over the ice cubes. For a lighter version of the drink, add the sparkling water.

Chocolate Martini

A chocoholic's dream, silky and smooth, to be drunk unapologetically in front of the martini purists who will undoubtedly scoff. Just don't let them taste it— you'll have to fight to get your glass back.

Serves 1

- **1 ounce Vanilla Vodka (page 34)**

- **1 ounce Chocolate Vodka (page 17)**

- **1 ounce plain vodka**

    Splash of Orange Vodka (page 18) or any commercial orange-flavored liqueur

- **1 cup cracked ice**

- **1 strawberry, whole or sliced**

Combine the vodkas and cracked ice in a shaker. Shake for 10 to 15 seconds, then strain into a chilled cocktail glass. Garnish with the strawberry slice.

Cosmopolitan

The *Sex and the City* girls gave new cachet to the pink and pretty cosmopolitan, the descendant of the sidecar and the Cape Codder. Like all drinks that become easy targets through popularity, it's a guilty pleasure that's much better than drink purists would have you believe.

2 ounces Orange Vodka (page 18)

1 ounce cranberry juice

1/2 ounce fresh lime juice

1 cup cracked ice

1 slice of orange

Combine the vodka, cranberry and lime juices, and cracked ice in a shaker. Shake for 10 to 15 seconds, then strain into a chilled cocktail glass. Garnish with the orange slice.

Cranberry-Orange Martini

Sweet, tart, and revitalizing with an intense fruity flavor—an infused variation of the cosmo.

Serves 1

1 **ounce Orange Vodka (page 18)**

1 **ounce Cranberry Vodka (page 15)**

1 **ounce plain vodka**

Splash of fresh lime juice

1 **cup cracked ice**

1 **slice of lime**

Combine the vodkas, lime juice, and cracked ice in a shaker. Shake for 10 to 15 seconds, then strain into a chilled cocktail glass. Garnish with the lime slice.

Cuba Libre

Much better than the traditional rum and Coca-Cola, this drink originated in 1900, right after the Spanish-American War—"Cuba libre!" was the rallying cry of the Cuban independence movement. The drink became popular during World War II, when Caribbean rum was one of the only spirits found in the United States (American alcohol was going to soldiers overseas). Sugar was rationed, but somehow Coca-Cola wasn't. Even if you think a rum and Coke is too sweet, give this drink a try—lime provides tartness for balance.

Serves 1

1/2   lime

4 or 5   ice cubes

2   ounces Lime Rum (page 18)

1/2   cup Coca-Cola, chilled

1   lime wedge

Squeeze the juice from the lime half into a chilled collins glass and add the ice cubes. Pour in the rum, then fill the glass with the Coca-Cola. Stir for 20 to 30 seconds and garnish with the lime wedge.

Depth Bomb

Serves 1

According to *The Savoy Cocktail Book* (1930), this drink owes its inspiration to the M. L. Submarine Chasers of World War I.

- **2** ounces brandy
- **2** ounces Apple Brandy (page 13)
- **1** teaspoon grenadine
- **2** teaspoons fresh lemon juice
- **1** cup cracked ice

Combine all the ingredients in a shaker. Shake for 10 to 15 seconds, then strain into a chilled old-fashioned glass.

Dirty Martini

Serves 1

The boozy classic has a lethal edge provided by Red Chile Vodka. It's said that FDR favored dirty martinis, heavy on the vermouth, considered most unfashionable.

- **2 1/2** ounces Red Chile Vodka (page 16)
- **1** ounce dry vermouth, or to taste
- **Brine from cocktail olives to taste**
- **1** cup cracked ice
- **1 to 3** cocktail olives

Combine the vodka, vermouth, olive brine, and cracked ice in a shaker. Shake for 10 to 15 seconds, then strain into a chilled cocktail glass. Garnish with one or more olives.

Earl Grey Martini

Lyrical and sophisticated, this martini is perfumed with Earl Grey tea's blend of Indian and Ceylon teas and bitter orange bergamot fragrance—a perfect pick-me-up cocktail.

Serves 1

- **2 ounces Earl Grey Tea Vodka (page 31)**
- **1 ounce plain vodka**
- **1 cup cracked ice**
- **1 lemon twist**

Combine the vodkas and cracked ice in a shaker. Shake for 10 to 15 seconds, then strain into a chilled cocktail glass. Garnish with the lemon twist.

Eastwind

An amber aperitif of classic ingredients, perfect before a sophisticated meal. Black Currant Vodka adds a French twist.

Serves 1

- **1 ounce Black Currant Vodka (page 15)**
- **1 ounce dry vermouth**
- **1 ounce sweet vermouth**
- **1 cup cracked ice**
- **1 lemon twist**

Combine the vodka, vermouths, and cracked ice in a shaker. Shake for 10 to 15 seconds, then strain into a chilled old-fashioned glass. Garnish with the lemon twist.

French Martini

A gorgeously seductive, rosy-hued alternative to the cosmo—and dangerously drinkable.

Serves 1

1 **ounce Raspberry Vodka (page 15)**

1/2 **ounce Orange Vodka or Orange Brandy (page 18)**

1 **ounce fresh orange juice**

1 **cup cracked ice**

Sparkling water or club soda to taste

1 **slice of orange**

Combine the vodkas, orange juice, and cracked ice in a shaker. Shake for 10 to 15 seconds, then strain into a chilled cocktail glass. Top off with sparkling water. Garnish with the orange slice.

Gazpacho Mary

This recipe, using vodka infused with tomatoes, chiles, cucumber, and onions, adds a depth and intensity of flavor to a classic Bloody Mary. A splash of Gazpacho Vodka is also delicious in gazpacho soup.

Serves 1

4 or 5	ice cubes
2	ounces Gazpacho Vodka (page 22)
1/2	cup tomato juice
1 1/2	teaspoons fresh lemon juice
	Splash of Worcestershire sauce
3 or 4	dashes of Tabasco sauce
	Pinch of salt
	Pinch of freshly ground pepper
1	celery stick
1	lemon wedge

Place the ice cubes in a chilled collins glass. Combine the vodka, tomato and lemon juices, and Worcestershire and Tabasco sauces in a shaker. Shake for 10 to 15 seconds, then strain over the ice cubes. Season with the salt and pepper, and garnish with the celery stick and lemon wedge.

Gibson

Serves 1

A spiky and acerbic cocktail attributed to Charles Dana Gibson, *Life* illustrator and creator of the "Gibson girl," and first served at the Plaza Hotel in New York.

2	ounces plain vodka
1/2	ounce Onion Vodka (page 22)
1/2	ounce dry vermouth, or to taste
1	cup cracked ice
1 or 2	cocktail onions

Combine the vodkas, vermouth, and cracked ice in a shaker. Shake for 10 to 15 seconds, then strain into a chilled cocktail glass. Garnish with 1 or 2 cocktail onions.

Ginger-Peach Martini

Serves 1

Vodka infused with ripe, luscious peaches adds summer sweetness, while tangy-hot Ginger Vodka provides bite.

1	ounce Peach Vodka (page 26)
1	ounce Ginger Vodka (page 30)
1	ounce plain vodka
1	cup cracked ice
1	piece of candied ginger

Combine the vodkas and cracked ice in a shaker. Shake for 10 to 15 seconds, then strain into a chilled cocktail glass. Garnish with the candied ginger.

Green Hat

The Green Hat was created at the Bar Cambon at the Ritz Paris (across from Bar Hemingway) in 1933. The combination of ingredients may sound old-fashioned, but the result is delightfully pungent and evocative. Have one and think of Jean Harlow in the 1933 film *Dinner at Eight.*

Serves 1

4 or 5	**ice cubes**
2	**ounces gin**
2	**ounces Peppermint Vodka (page 23)**
1	**ounce club soda**

Place the ice cubes in a chilled collins glass. Pour the remaining ingredients over the ice cubes, then stir for 10 to 15 seconds.

Hot Toddy

The spicy and delicious Hot Toddy is good for a cold night and for a head cold.

Serves 1

	Splash of fresh lemon juice
2	**teaspoons honey or sugar**
2	**ounces Spiced Rum (page 30)**
1/2	**cup hot water**
1	**cinnamon stick**

In a preheated mug, mix together the lemon juice and honey. Add the rum, then top off with the hot water. Stir with the cinnamon stick, leaving it in the drink for garnish.

Jade Blossom Martini

A subtle and sophisticated cocktail that features the flavors of cooling cucumber, tangy lime, and fragrant green tea.

Serves 1

1   **ounce Cucumber Vodka (page 20)**

1   **ounce Lime Vodka (page 18)**

1   **ounce Green Tea Vodka (page 31)**

1   **cup cracked ice**

1   **thin slice of cucumber**

Combine the vodkas and cracked ice in a shaker. Shake for 10 to 15 seconds, then strain into a chilled cocktail glass. Garnish with the cucumber slice.

Jack O'Lantern

A terrific Halloween cocktail. Serve as an aperitif or with dessert through the month of October.

Serves 1

6 to 8   **pumpkin seeds**

1   **ounce Pumpkin Vodka (page 29)**

1   **ounce Spiced Vodka (page 30)**

1   **ounce Maker's Mark or other bourbon**

Juice of 1/2 lemon

1   **cup cracked ice**

Heat a large, heavy skillet over medium heat until hot. Add the pumpkin seeds and toast, stirring constantly, until they expand and begin to pop, 3 to 5 minutes. Transfer to a plate to cool.

Combine the vodkas, bourbon, lemon juice, and cracked ice in a shaker. Shake for 10 to 15 seconds, then strain into a cocktail glass. Garnish with the toasted pumpkin seeds.

Lemon Drop

Citron pressé for grown-ups—infused lemon and orange vodkas make this version of the sweet-and-sour lemon drop memorable.

Serves 1

- 1   **lemon wedge**

    Sugar

- 2   **ounces Lemon Vodka (page 18)**

- 1   **ounce Orange Vodka (page 18)**

    Splash of fresh lime juice

- 1   **cup cracked ice**

    Splash of lemon-lime soda, sparkling water, or club soda

- 1   **slice of lemon**

Rub the rim of a chilled cocktail glass with the lemon wedge, then dip it in the sugar to coat. Combine the vodkas, lime juice, and cracked ice in a shaker. Shake well for 10 to 15 seconds, then strain into the glass. Top off with the lemon-lime soda and garnish with the lemon slice.

Lavender Martini

Serves 1

Lavender is often used as a spice in the south of France. Here it adds a distinctively clean herbal note, evoking hot blue summers in Provençe.

1   ounce Vanilla Vodka (page 34)

2   ounces Lavender Vodka (page 21)

    Splash of fresh lemon juice

1   cup cracked ice

    Sparkling water or club soda

8 to 10   fresh or dried organically grown lavender buds
          or 1 fresh mint leaf

Combine the vodkas, lemon juice, and cracked ice in a shaker. Shake for 10 to 15 seconds, then strain into a chilled cocktail glass. Top with sparkling water. Garnish with the lavender buds.

Lemon Melon

Serves 1

The Lemon Vodka makes this drink sharp and tangy, while the Midori, a melon liqueur, adds sweetness without being cloying. This drink is perfect for a summer party.

4 or 5   **ice cubes**

1   **ounce Lemon Vodka (page 18)**

1   **ounce Midori**

1/2   **cup sparkling water or club soda**

1   **thin slice of melon, such as cantaloupe or honeydew**

Place the ice cubes in a chilled collins glass. Pour the vodka and Midori over the ice cubes, then stir for 20 to 30 seconds. Top off with the sparkling water and garnish with the melon slice.

NOTE: Melon is one of the few fruits that doesn't infuse well; it's better to use Midori.

Lemon Sambuca Martini

Lemon provides tartness, while sambuca, an Italian anise-flavored liqueur, adds sweetness and sophistication.

Serves 1

- 3 **ounces Lemon Vodka (page 18)**
- 1/2 **ounce sambuca**
- 1 **cup cracked ice**
- 1 **lemon twist**

Combine the vodka, sambuca, and cracked ice in a shaker. Shake well for 10 to 15 seconds, then strain into a chilled cocktail glass. Garnish with the lemon twist.

Lime Gin and Tonic

This summertime classic tastes even more tart and fresh with Lime Gin (or vodka, for that matter).

Serves 1

- 4 or 5 **ice cubes**
- 2 **ounces Lime Gin (page 18)**
- 1/2 **cup tonic water**
- 1 **lime wedge**

Place the ice cubes in a chilled collins glass. Add the gin. Top off with the tonic and garnish with the lime wedge.

Lime Rickey

An infused twist on the drugstore classic—rumored to have been one of Elvis's favorites.

4 or 5 ice cubes

2 ounces Lime Gin (page 18)

Dash of grenadine (optional)

1/2 well-scrubbed lime

Up to 1 ounce sugar syrup (page 11; optional)

1/2 cup sparkling water or club soda

1 thin slice of lime

Place the ice cubes in a chilled collins glass. Pour in the gin and grenadine (if desired), squeeze the juice from the lime half into the glass and drop in the lime shell. Add the sugar syrup (if desired), then stir for 20 to 30 seconds. Top off with the sparkling water and garnish with the lime slice.

Lychee Martini

Lychee-infused vodka adds an unexpectedly exotic and glamorous touch to a martini.

Serves 1

- **1 ounce plain vodka**
- **2 ounces Lychee Vodka (page 24)**
- **Splash of fresh lemon juice**
- **1 cup cracked ice**
- **Sparkling water or club soda**
- **1 fresh lychee or 1 lemon twist**

Combine the vodkas, lemon juice, and the cracked ice in a shaker. Shake for 10 to 15 seconds, then strain into a chilled cocktail glass. Top off with sparkling water and garnish with the lychee.

Lychee Sour

A sweet-sharp cocktail with an exotic twist.

Serves 1

- **2 ounces Lychee Vodka (page 24)**
- **1 ounce plain vodka**
- **Juice of 1/2 lemon**
- **1 teaspoon sugar syrup (page 11)**
- **1 cup cracked ice**
- **1 thin slice of lychee**

Combine the vodkas, lemon juice, sugar syrup, and cracked ice in a shaker. Shake for 10 to 15 seconds, then strain into a chilled cocktail glass. Garnish with the lychee slice.

Madras

The essence of summer in a glass, the classic madras (named after the colorful plaid worn by preppies) is a descendant of the Cape Codder and the forerunner of the ubiquitous cosmopolitan. It's even more delicious made with infused vodkas.

Serves 1

4 or 5   ice cubes

1   ounce Orange Vodka or Orange Rum (page 18)

1   ounce Cranberry Vodka or Cranberry Rum (page 15)

2   ounces fresh orange juice

2   ounces cranberry juice

Splash of sparkling water or club soda

1   orange or lime wedge

Place the ice cubes in a chilled collins glass. Pour in the vodkas and the orange and cranberry juices. Top off with the sparkling water and garnish with the citrus wedge.

Mangopolitan

Serves 1

A seductive and urbane alternative to the cosmopolitan, using Mango Vodka. A great prelude to a spicy Indian feast.

2   ounces Mango Vodka (page 25)

1   ounce plain vodka

2   tablespoons mango purée

Juice of 1/2 lime

1   cup cracked ice

1   mango slice

Combine the vodkas, mango purée, lime juice, and cracked ice in a shaker. Shake for 10 to 15 seconds, then strain into a chilled cocktail glass. Garnish with the mango slice.

Mango Purée

1   mango, peeled and pitted

1/4   cup sugar or to taste

1/2   teaspoon fresh lemon juice

Combine the mango, sugar, and lemon juice in a food processor. Process until smooth.

Margarita

A variation on the classic sidecar, the margarita was first mentioned in the 1937 *Café Royal Cocktail Book,* but came into its own in the 1970s. It's worth squeezing your own lime juice for maximum tang and tartness.

Serves 1

1 **lime wedge**

Coarse salt

2 **ounces Lime Tequila (page 18)**

1 **ounce Cointreau**

1 **ounce fresh lime juice**

1 **cup cracked ice**

Rub the rim of a chilled cocktail glass with the lime wedge, then dip it in the coarse salt to coat. Combine the remaining ingredients in a shaker. Shake well for 10 to 15 seconds, then strain into the glass.

Madame Mona

The origins of the Madame Mona are lost to mixology history but the cocktail is delicious. Drink it and perfect your Mona Lisa smile.

1 ounce Lavender Vodka (page 21)

1 ounce Orange Vodka (page 18) or Cointreau

1 ounce cranberry juice

1 cup cracked ice

Combine the vodkas, cranberry juice, and cracked ice in a shaker. Shake for 10 to 15 seconds, then strain into a chilled cocktail glass.

Mint Julep

The favored drink of the Kentucky Derby, the mint julep has as many recipes as good ol' boys (and girls) to make them. Whatever time of year you choose to enjoy this cocktail, the Mint Bourbon evokes a hot summer afternoon on Jay Gatsby's manicured lawn.

3 ounces Mint Bourbon (page 23)

1 teaspoon sugar syrup (page 11)

3 mint sprigs

1 cup cracked ice

In a chilled silver julep cup (if you didn't inherit grand-daddy's, try a chilled old-fashioned glass), pour in the bourbon and sugar syrup and stir gently. Add 2 mint sprigs and the cracked ice. Garnish with the remaining mint sprig. Let stand for 5 minutes before serving.

Moscow Mule

Right before World War II, Jack Morgan, owner of the Cock 'n' Bull pub in Hollywood, had a problem—too much ginger beer on his hands. The solution? An invigorating cocktail with a catchy name.

Serves 1

- 1/2 **well-scrubbed lime**
- **4 or 5 ice cubes**
- 2 **ounces Lime Vodka (page 18)**
- 1/2 **cup ginger beer or ginger ale**
- 1 **lime wedge**

Squeeze the juice from the lime half into a chilled collins glass and drop in the lime shell. Add the ice cubes, pour in the vodka, and top off with the ginger beer. Give a few stirs and garnish with the lime wedge.

Provençal Lemonade

Redolent of the summer-scented countryside of southern France. Peter Mayle would approve.

Serves 1

- 2 **ounces Lavender Vodka (page 21)**
- **4 or 5 ice cubes**
- 1/2 **cup lemonade, preferably freshly made**
- 1 **lemon wedge**

Pour the vodka into a chilled collins glass. Add the ice cubes, then top off with the lemonade. Give a few stirs and garnish with the lemon wedge.

Paloma

Serves 1

More popular in Mexico than the margarita, the paloma is refined, lighter, and more refreshing. The bartender at the Camino Real Hotel in Mexico City makes a great one.

- **1 lime wedge**

   Coarse salt

- **2 ounces Grapefruit Tequila (page 18)**

- **1 ounce fresh lime juice**

- **6 drops hot sauce, such as Tabasco (optional)**

- **1 cup cracked ice**

- **1/2 cup grapefruit-flavored soda, such as Fresca**

Rub the rim of a chilled cocktail glass with the lime wedge, then dip it in the coarse salt to coat. Combine the tequila, lime juice, hot sauce (if desired), and cracked ice in a shaker. Shake for 10 to 15 seconds, then strain into the glass. Top off with the soda.

Pear Martini with Lemon and Rosemary

Pear Brandy gives the drink sweetness, fresh lemon juice tartness, and Rosemary Vodka an unexpected herbal twist.

Serves 1

 1 **ounce plain vodka**

 1/2 **ounce Rosemary Vodka (page 23)**

 1 **ounce Pear Brandy (page 27)**

 1 **teaspoon fresh lemon juice**

 1 **cup cracked ice**

 1 **rosemary sprig**

Combine the vodkas, brandy, lemon juice, and cracked ice in a shaker. Shake for 10 to 15 seconds, then strain into a chilled cocktail glass. Garnish with the rosemary sprig.

Piña Colada

Serves 1

The creamy and luscious cocktail has a questionable reputation but an impeccable pedigree—Ramon Marrero Perez claims to have invented the piña colada in 1954, while Don Ramon Portas Mingot is said to have invented it in Puerto Rico in 1963. Have one while watching the sunset from a deck chair and then decide for yourself. Coconut shells for serving are optional.

2	ounces Coconut Rum (page 32)
3	ounces unsweetened pineapple juice, preferably fresh
1	ounce coconut cream, such as Coco López
5 or 6	ice cubes
1	small pineapple wedge
1	maraschino cherry

Combine the rum, pineapple juice, and coconut cream in a blender and process on high. Add the ice cubes, one at a time, and process until smooth. Pour into a chilled Bordeaux glass. Garnish with everything you've got—pineapple wedge, maraschino cherry, perhaps a little umbrella.

Pink Ginger Lemonade

Perfect for a picnic—sunshiny and sweet, with just a touch of unexpected spicy heat.

Serves 1

2	ounces Ginger Vodka (page 30)
4 or 5	ice cubes
1/2	cup pink lemonade, preferably freshly made
1	lemon wedge

Pour the vodka into a chilled collins glass. Add the ice cubes, then top off with the lemonade. Give a few stirs and garnish with the lemon wedge.

Pink Grapefruit Margarita

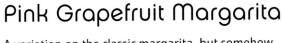

A variation on the classic margarita, but somehow lighter and mellower with grapefruit-infused white tequila.

Serves 1

- **1 lime wedge**
- **Sugar**
- **2 ounces Grapefruit Tequila (page 18)**
- **1 ounce Cointreau**
- **1 ounce fresh pink grapefruit juice**
- **1 cup cracked ice**

Rub the rim of a chilled cocktail glass with the lime wedge, then dip it into the sugar to coat. Combine the remaining ingredients in a shaker. Shake for 10 to 15 seconds, then strain into the glass.

Raspberry Beret

A drink fit for a Prince.

Serves 1

2 ounces Raspberry Vodka (page 15)

1 ounce plain vodka

1 cup cracked ice

1 to 3 raspberries

Combine the vodkas and cracked ice in a shaker. Shake for 10 to 15 seconds, then strain into a chilled cocktail glass. Garnish with the raspberries.

Red Chile Bloody Maria

A variation on the classic Bloody Mary, using red chile–infused tequila for the perfect touch of searing heat.

Serves 1

4 or 5	ice cubes
2	ounces Red Chile Tequila (page 16)
1/2	cup tomato juice
1 1/2	teaspoons fresh lemon juice
	Splash of Worcestershire sauce
3 or 4	dashes of Tabasco sauce
1	lemon wedge

Place the ice cubes in a chilled collins glass. Combine the tequila, tomato and lemon juices, and Worcestershire and Tabasco sauces in a shaker. Shake for 10 to 15 seconds, then strain over the ice cubes. Garnish with the lemon wedge.

Rose Petal Martini

Rosy, sweet, and unabashedly pretty, this is the perfect drink for a summer wedding.

Serves 1

- **2 ounces Rose Vodka (page 21)**
- **1 ounce Vanilla Vodka (page 34)**
- **Splash of cranberry juice**
- **1 cup cracked ice**
- **1 candied rose petal**

Combine the vodkas, cranberry juice, and cracked ice in a shaker. Shake for 10 to 15 seconds, then strain into a chilled cocktail glass. Garnish with the rose petal.

Candied Rose Petals

1 extra-large egg white, at room temperature

A few drops of water

1 cup superfine sugar

Organically grown rose petals, rinsed and dried

In a small bowl, combine the egg white and water. Beat lightly with a small whisk until the egg white shows a few bubbles. Place the sugar in a saucer or shallow bowl.

Dip a small paintbrush into the egg mixture and gently paint both sides of each petal. Cover the petal completely but sparingly. Sprinkle the sugar evenly on both sides of the petal, shaking off any excess. Place on wax paper to dry.

Let the petals dry completely, from 12 to 36 hours, depending on the humidity. Or place the candied petals on a baking sheet in an oven set at 150°F to 200°F with the door ajar for 2 to 3 hours.

Store the candied petals in an airtight container for up to 1 year.

Rosemary Martini

This cocktail was inspired by Gramercy Tavern's rosma-rino, concocted by master mixologist Nick Mauntone. Here, rosemary-infused vodka lends a bittersweet, lemony, slightly piney essence, and mixes nicely with the anise flavor of the Pernod, a French liqueur.

3   **ounces Rosemary Vodka (page 23)**

1/2   **ounce dry vermouth, or to taste**

    Splash of Pernod

1   **cup cracked ice**

1   **rosemary sprig**

Combine the vodka, vermouth, Pernod, and cracked ice in a shaker. Shake for 10 to 15 seconds, then strain into a chilled cocktail glass. Garnish with the rosemary sprig.

ſidecar

The decadent orange-perfumed sidecar is rumored to have been created at Harry's New York Bar in Paris in 1931. It was a favorite of the literary expat crowd. Drink a toast to Hemingway, F. Scott, and Gertrude.

Serves 1

- 1 **lemon wedge**
- **Sugar**
- 1 **ounce plain brandy**
- 1/2 **ounce Orange Brandy (page 18)**
- **Juice of 1/2 lemon**
- 1 **cup cracked ice**

Rub the rim of a chilled cocktail glass with the lemon wedge, then dip it in the sugar to coat. Combine the remaining ingredients in a shaker. Shake for 10 to 15 seconds, then strain into the glass.

Singapore Sling

The Raffles Hotel in Singapore is the birthplace of
the Singapore sling. The 1915 formula was created
by Ngiam Tong Boon, of the Raffles Hotel's Long Bar.
A drink where "less is more" does not apply—bring
on the paper umbrellas and straws!

Serves 1

2	ounces gin
1/2	ounce Cherry Brandy (page 15)
1/2	ounce Bénédictine
1/2	ounce fresh lemon juice
1	teaspoon sugar syrup (optional; page 11)
1	cup cracked ice
2 or 3	ounces sparkling water or club soda
3	maraschino cherries and slices of fresh fruit, such as pineapple

Combine the gin, brandy, Bénédictine, lemon juice, sugar
syrup (if desired), and cracked ice in a shaker. Shake for 10
to 15 seconds, then strain into a chilled Bordeaux glass.
Top off with sparkling water. Garnish with the maraschino
cherries and fresh fruit.

Tangerine Dream

A gorgeous drink, evocative of fiery orange-red sunsets. Tangerine is an unexpected alternative to orange, while the Campari, an Italian aperitif made according to a secret recipe developed in 1860 by Gaspare Campari in Milan, adds a bittersweet note.

1	ounce Tangerine Vodka (page 18)
1	ounce plain vodka
1/2	ounce Campari
1/2	ounce fresh tangerine juice
1	cup cracked ice
1	tangerine twist

Combine the vodkas, Campari, tangerine juice, and cracked ice in a shaker. Shake for 10 to 15 seconds, then strain into a chilled cocktail glass. Garnish with the tangerine twist.

Strawberry Basil Martini

A refreshing and unusual aperitif, ideal for summer garden parties. The Strawberry Vodka provides sweetness, while the unexpected leafy note of basil undercuts it nicely.

Serves 1

- **1 ounce Strawberry Vodka (page 15)**
- **1 ounce Basil Vodka (page 23)**
- **1 ounce plain vodka**
- **1 cup cracked ice**
- **Splash of sparkling water or club soda**
- **1 strawberry or 1 basil leaf**

Combine the vodkas and cracked ice in a shaker. Shake for 10 to 15 seconds, then strain into a chilled cocktail glass. Top off with the sparkling water and garnish with the strawberry.

Tokyo Martini

An unusual and exotic combination of tastes—
Cucumber Vodka is cooling and slightly sweet, while
sake, a Japanese white wine made from fermented rice,
is smooth and crisp. Pretend you're at Tokyo's Park
Hyatt Hotel, overlooking the lights of the city at night.

Serves 1

1   **ounce sake**

2   **ounces Cucumber Vodka (page 20)**

1   **cup cracked ice**

1   **thin slice of cucumber**

Combine the sake, vodka, and cracked ice in a shaker.
Shake for 10 to 15 seconds, then strain into a chilled
cocktail glass. Garnish with the cucumber slice.

Vanilla Coke

A variation on the rum and Coke, this infused version
is a soda-bar favorite made for grown-ups. Try it with
fried peanut-butter-and-banana sandwiches and Elvis's
"King Creole" playing on the stereo.

Serves 1

4 or 5   **ice cubes**

2   **ounces Vanilla Rum or Vanilla Vodka (page 34)**

1/2   **cup Coca-Cola, chilled**

Place the ice cubes in a chilled collins glass. Pour in the
rum. Top off with the Coca-Cola.

Vanilla Julep

A voluptuous vanilla-infused twist on the classic mint julep. Just what Daisy Buchanan might have sipped on Jay Gatsby's lawn.

Serves 1

1   ounce plain vodka

    Dash of fresh lime juice

    Dash of sugar syrup (page 11; optional)

3   mint sprigs

1   cup cracked ice

2   ounces Vanilla Bourbon (page 34)

Combine the vodka, lime juice, and sugar syrup (if desired) in a shaker. Add 2 of the mint sprigs and the cracked ice. Pour in the bourbon and stir, gently bruising the leaves. Strain into a chilled cocktail glass. Garnish with the remaining mint sprig.

Vesper

An orange-infused twist on one of James Bond's favorite cocktails. The recipe is included in Ian Fleming's *Casino Royale*. In the novel, Bond creates the recipe and teaches it to the barman: "In a deep champagne goblet. . . . Three measures of Gordon's, one of vodka, half a measure of Kina Lillet. Shake it very well until it's ice-cold, then add a large thin slice of lemon peel." Bond named his special martini after female double agent Vesper Lynd. Lillet Blanc, a blend of white wines, herbs, and fruit, is a perfect complement to Orange Vodka and gin.

- **3 ounces gin**
- **1 ounce Orange Vodka (page 18)**
- **1/2 ounce Lillet Blanc, or to taste**
- **1 cup cracked ice**
- **1 lemon twist or 1 slice of orange**

Combine the gin, vodka, Lillet Blanc, and cracked ice in a shaker. Shake for 10 to 15 seconds, then strain into a chilled cocktail glass. Garnish with the lemon twist.

Vin d'Orange

This infused version of a fruity French favorite is terrific served cold, with lots of ice.

Serves 1

- **4 or 5**   **ice cubes**
- **1**   **ounce Orange Brandy (page 18)**
- **3**   **ounces dry white wine, such as white Bordeaux or Riesling**
- **1**   **slice of orange**
- **1**   **slice of lemon**

Place the ice cubes in a Bordeaux glass. Pour in the brandy and wine and stir. Garnish with the orange and lemon slices.

Vermouth Cassis

Known in France as the *pompier* (fireman), this drink became popular in New York in the 1930s. It's an elegant aperitif, the sort of cocktail Jean Gabin might have ordered at a café on Île St-Louis.

Serves 1

- **3**   **ounces dry vermouth**
- **1/2**   **ounce Black Currant Vodka (page 15)**
- **4 or 5**   **ice cubes**
- **2 to 3**   **ounces sparkling water or club soda**

Pour the vermouth and vodka into a chilled collins glass. Add the ice cubes. Top off with the sparkling water.

Violet Vodka Martini

Serves 1

Crowned with an edible flower, the Violet Martini, with its amethyst hue, looks as divine as it tastes.

- **1 ounce Violet Vodka (page 21)**
- **1 ounce plain vodka**
- **1/2 ounce Cointreau**
- **1/2 ounce Grand Marnier**
- **Splash of cranberry juice**
- **Splash of lime juice**
- **1 cup cracked ice**
- **1 candied violet or 1 mint leaf**

Combine the vodkas, Cointreau, Grand Marnier, cranberry and lime juices, and cracked ice in a shaker. Shake for 10 to 15 seconds, then strain into a chilled cocktail glass. Garnish with the candied violet or mint leaf.

Candied Violets

1 extra-large egg white, at room temperature

A few drops of water

1 cup superfine sugar

Organically grown violets, stems removed, rinsed and patted dry

In a small bowl, combine the egg white and water. Beat lightly with a small whisk until the egg white shows a few bubbles. Place the sugar in a saucer or shallow bowl.

Dip a small paintbrush into the egg mixture and gently paint both sides of each flower. Cover the flower completely but sparingly. Sprinkle the sugar evenly on both sides of the flower, shaking off any excess. Place on wax paper to dry.

Candied Violets (continued)

Let the flowers dry completely, from 12 to 36 hours, depending on the humidity. Or place the candied flowers on a baking sheet in an oven set at 150°F to 200°F with the door ajar for 2 to 3 hours.

Store the candied flowers in an airtight container for up to 1 year.

Zelda

A fiery cocktail inspired by Zelda Fitzgerald, free-spirited writer, Southern belle, and F. Scott's wife, served at the Ritz Paris.

Serves 1

1/2   **cup Red Chile Tequila (page 16)**

2   **ounces fresh lemon juice**

1   **cup cracked ice**

1   **lemon wedge**

Combine the tequila, lemon juice, and cracked ice in a shaker. Shake for 10 to 15 seconds, then strain into a chilled old-fashioned glass. Garnish with the lemon wedge.

Wasabi Mary

The following Thai-chile-pepper-infused variation of the Bloody Mary is unorthodox, but still contains the classic components: spirits, tomato and citrus juices, salt, and spice. The soy sauce and wasabi provide unexpected bite and heat.

4 or 5	ice cubes
2	ounces Thai Chile Vodka (page 16)
1/2	cup tomato juice
1 1/2	teaspoons fresh lime juice
	Splash of soy sauce
1/2	teaspoon wasabi paste, or to taste
	Pinch of salt
1	slice of pickled ginger
1	lime wedge

Place the ice cubes in a chilled collins glass. Combine the vodka, tomato and lime juices, soy sauce, wasabi, and salt in a shaker. Shake for 10 to 15 seconds, then strain into the glass. Garnish with the ginger slice and lime wedge.

Watermelon Martini

Summertime, when the livin' is easy and the watermelons are sweet and juicy, is the right time to make this delightful juicy-pink cocktail.

Serves 1

2 ounces watermelon purée

2 ounces Watermelon Vodka (page 35)

1 cup cracked ice

1 thin slice of watermelon

Combine the watermelon purée, vodka, and cracked ice in a shaker and shake for 10 to 15 seconds. Strain into a chilled cocktail glass and garnish with the watermelon slice.

Watermelon Purée

1/2 cup cubed watermelon

1/2 teaspoon fresh lemon juice

In a small bowl, crush the watermelon with a fork until it reaches the desired consistency. Add the lemon juice and stir.

Zendo Rosemary Cider

Serves 1

Dai Bosatu Zendo, a Zen monastery in upstate New York, makes a nonalcoholic version of this drink. But for those of us who are not Zen monks, the addition of rosemary-infused vodka is a lovely and unexpected touch. The drink is also delicious served hot.

4 to 5	ice cubes
1	ounce Rosemary Vodka (page 23)
1	ounce plain vodka
1	cup cracked ice
1/2	cup fresh-pressed nonalcoholic apple cider
1	rosemary sprig

Place the ice cubes in a chilled collins glass. Combine the vodkas and cracked ice in a shaker. Shake for 10 to 15 seconds, then strain over the ice cubes. Top off with the apple cider. Garnish with the rosemary sprig.

Champagne Cocktails

Arise My Love

A classic Champagne cocktail with a Psalms-inspired name. The mint flavor of the vodka adds a sharp sweetness to the Champagne.

- 1/2 ounce Mint Vodka (page 23)
- 1/2 cup chilled sparkling wine or Champagne
- 1 mint leaf or 1 slice of orange

Pour the vodka into a chilled champagne flute. Top off with the sparkling wine. Garnish with the fresh mint leaf

Serves 1

Aztec

An unexpected, sweet Mexican twist on the Champagne cocktail.

- 1 ounce Watermelon Tequila (page 35)
- 1/2 cup chilled sparkling wine or Champagne
- 1 small slice of watermelon

Pour the tequila into a chilled champagne flute. Top off with the sparkling wine. Garnish with the watermelon slice.

Serves 1

Champagne Charlie

A classic cocktail, traditionally made with Charles Heidsieck Champagne. Apricot Brandy adds a sweet richness to the fizz.

Ice cubes

1 ounce Apricot Brandy (page 14)

1/2 cup chilled sparkling wine or Champagne

1/2 slice of orange

Half fill a chilled champagne flute with ice cubes. Pour in the brandy. Top off with the sparkling wine. Garnish with the orange slice.

The Churchill

Sir Winston invented this one himself, according to the 1965 *Esquire Party Book*. Note the ratio of Orange Brandy to Champagne—Churchill's favorite was Pol Roget.

3 ounces Orange Brandy (page 18)

1 1/2 ounces chilled sparkling wine or Champagne

Pour the brandy into a chilled old-fashioned glass. Top off with the sparkling wine.

Corpse Reviver

Another drink attributed to Papa Hemingway. The drops of tangy, freshly squeezed lemon juice are integral to the drink's balance.

Serves 1

3/4   ounce Anise Vodka (page 30)

1/2   cup chilled sparkling wine or Champagne

3 or 4   drops of fresh lemon juice

Pour the vodka into a chilled champagne flute. Top off with the sparkling wine, then sprinkle with the lemon juice.

Elderflower Royale

An elegant summer cocktail. The dry Champagne offsets the floral sweetness of the elderflower-infused vodka.

Serves 1

1   ounce Elderflower Vodka (page 21)

1/2   cup chilled sparkling wine or Champagne

Pour the vodka into a chilled champagne flute. Top off with the sparkling wine.

Ginger Champagne Cocktail

An elegant aperitif with a spicy-hot kick.

Serves 1

   1   **ounce Ginger Vodka (page 30)**

  1/2 **cup chilled sparkling wine or Champagne**

Pour the vodka into a chilled champagne flute. Top off with the sparkling wine.

Lychee Fizz

No one seems to know where this ambrosial drink was invented, but Bar Aldwych in London makes a terrific one, perfumed with the delicate sweetness of lychee.

Serves 1

   1   **ounce Lychee Vodka (page 24)**

  1/2 **cup chilled sparkling wine or Champagne**

   1   **fresh lychee or 1 lemon twist**

Pour the vodka into a chilled champagne flute. Top off with the sparkling wine. Garnish with the lychee.

Poinsettia

A festive, garnet-colored holiday cocktail served at the legendary Brown Derby in Los Angeles.

Serves 1

1	ounce Orange Vodka or Orange Brandy (page 18)
1	ounce cranberry juice
3	ounces chilled sparkling wine or Champagne
2 or 3	cranberries or 1 slice of orange

Pour the vodka into a chilled champagne flute. Add the cranberry juice. Top off with the sparkling wine. Garnish with the cranberries.

Poire Williams

In France, pear brandy is traditionally made with poire williams pears, and adds a summer-scented sweetness to the Champagne.

Serves 1

1	ounce Pear Brandy (page 27)
1/2	cup chilled sparkling wine or Champagne

Pour the brandy into a chilled champagne flute. Top off with the sparkling wine.

Rossini

Like a Bellini, but with strawberries instead of white peaches.

Serves 1

2 tablespoons chilled strawberry purée

1 ounce Strawberry Vodka (page 15)

3 ounces Prosecco or other sparkling wine

1 strawberry

Place the strawberry purée in a chilled champagne flute. Add the vodka. Top off slowly with the Prosecco (it has a tendency to foam). Garnish with the strawberry.

Strawberry Purée

4 or 5 fresh strawberries

1/2 teaspoon fresh lemon juice (optional)

1/2 teaspoon sugar (optional)

In a small bowl, crush the strawberries with a fork until puréed. Add the lemon juice and sugar, if desired, and stir. Chill for 1 hour before using. Store in the refrigerator for up to 24 hours.

Rose Kiss

Romance in a glass.

Serves 1

1 **ounce Rose Vodka (page 21)**

1/2 **cup chilled sparkling wine or Champagne**

1 **fresh organically grown rose petal or candied rose petal (page 89)**

Pour the vodka into a chilled champagne flute. Top off with the sparkling wine. Garnish with the rose petal.

Raspberry Fizz

An elegant rosy-hued aperitif. The lambent stained-glass hue of the Raspberry Vodka looks beautiful in candlelight.

Serves 1

1 **ounce Raspberry Vodka (page 15)**

1/2 **cup chilled sparkling wine or Champagne**

Pour the vodka into a chilled champagne flute. Top off with the sparkling wine.

Shy Violet

Violet Vodka adds a distinctive Victorian floral note.

Serves 1

1/2 **ounce Violet Vodka (page 21)**

1/2 **ounce Vanilla Vodka (page 34)**

3 **ounces chilled sparkling wine or Champagne**

1 **candied violet (page 102)**

Pour the vodkas into a chilled champagne flute. Top off with the sparkling wine and garnish with the violet.

Drinks for a Crowd

Brandy Punch

Serves 18

A traditional punch updated with orange-infused vodka, inspired by a recipe in *Esquire*'s 1949 *Handbook for Hosts*. The addition of grenadine, a sweet ruby-red pomegranate syrup, makes it especially festive.

1	**cup Orange Vodka or Orange Brandy (page 18)**
1/2	**cup fresh orange juice**
1/2	**ounce grenadine (optional)**
1	**cup fresh lemon juice, or to taste**
1	**cup superfine sugar**
1	**quart plain brandy**
	Large block of ice
1-liter	**bottle of sparkling water or club soda**
4	**lemons, scrubbed thoroughly and cut into thick slices**

Chill all the liquid ingredients. In a large bowl, mix together the vodka, orange juice, grenadine (if desired), and lemon juice. Stir in the sugar to taste. Add the plain brandy and chill for 2 to 3 hours. Place the ice in a punch bowl. Pour in the punch and add the sparkling water. Garnish with the lemon slices.

Champagne Punch

This beautiful, citrus-perfumed punch is ideal for a wedding, graduation, or brunch.

Serves 16

One 750-ml	**bottle of brut Champagne or sparkling wine**
1	**cup Orange Brandy or Orange Vodka (page 18)**
1-liter	**bottle of club soda or sparkling water**
	Large block of ice
1	**orange, scrubbed thoroughly and cut into thin slices**
	Fresh mint leaves

Chill all the liquid ingredients. In a large bowl, mix together the Champagne, brandy, and club soda. Place the ice in a punch bowl. Pour in the punch and garnish with the orange slices and mint.

Eggnog

Eggnog is a long-standing holiday tradition—and looking at the ingredients, it's probably a good thing that the drink is consumed only once a year. This recipe was inspired by Hillary Clinton's rich and creamy White House version.

Serves 22

4 **large organic eggs, separated**

1 **cup superfine sugar**

1/2 **cup plus 2 tablespoons bourbon**

1/2 **cup plus 2 tablespoons Cognac**

1/2 **cup plus 2 tablespoons Spiced Rum (page 30)**

1/2 **teaspoon salt**

2 **cups heavy cream**

1 **teaspoon vanilla extract**

1 **quart whole milk**

1/2 **teaspoon freshly grated nutmeg**

In a bowl, using an electric mixer on medium speed, beat the egg yolks while slowly adding the sugar. Continue to beat until the sugar is dissolved. Slowly pour in the bourbon, Cognac, and rum. Blend the ingredients with the mixer on low speed.

Place the egg whites in a large, clean bowl. Sprinkle with the salt. Using the mixer and clean beaters, beat on high speed until soft peaks form. In a separate bowl, whip the cream and vanilla on high speed until soft peaks form. Fold the egg yolk mixture into the egg whites, then fold in the whipped cream. Add the milk and mix well.

Chill the eggnog for 2 to 3 hours. Just before serving, whisk it to form foam on the surface. Sprinkle with the nutmeg.

NOTE: This recipe contains raw eggs. If you're unsure of the safety record of your egg provider, or you're serving people with compromised immune systems, do not make this recipe.

Glögg

Serves
28

Hot, spicy, and sweet, glögg is a traditional drink of the Swedish and Finnish Advent season—the four weeks leading up to Christmas.

4	cardamom pods
1/4	cup broken cinnamon sticks
25	whole cloves
	Zest of 1 well-scrubbed orange, cut into strips
Two 750-ml	bottles of dry red wine, such as Burgundy or Côtes du Rhone
One 750-ml	bottle of ruby port
1 1/2	cups raisins
1	cup blanched almonds
2	cups superfine sugar
1	quart Orange Brandy or Orange Vodka (page 18)

Remove the seeds from the cardamom pods and place the seeds, cinnamon, cloves, and orange zest on a square of cheesecloth. Bring up the corners and tie with kitchen string to form a bundle. In a large pot, combine the wine, port, raisins, almonds, and spice bundle. Simmer over medium heat until heated through, 15 to 20 minutes (do not boil).

In a wide saucepan, mix together the sugar and 1 cup of the brandy. Using a long-handled match, ignite the brandy. When the sugar has melted and the flames are extinguished, add the remaining brandy. Pour into the wine mixture. Remove and discard the spice bundle. Ladle the glögg into mugs.

Mulled Wine

A favorite in Victorian times, mulled (meaning "spiced") wine is a piping-hot holiday alternative to eggnog.

Serves 8

3 whole nutmegs

One 750-ml bottle of red wine, such as Burgundy or Côtes du Rhone

1 cup Orange Brandy or Orange Vodka (page 18)

2 lemons, scrubbed thoroughly and sliced

2 oranges, scrubbed thoroughly and sliced

13 cinnamon sticks, 5 broken into about three pieces each and 8 whole for garnish

1/2 to 1 cup sugar, or to taste

2 tablespoons whole cloves

Using a nutcracker, crack the whole nutmegs into pieces. (Or place them in a plastic bag and crack with a mallet.) Pour the wine into a large saucepan and gradually heat over medium heat. Add the brandy, lemon and orange slices, cinnamon pieces, nutmeg, sugar, and cloves. Keep an eye on the mixture—don't let it boil. Using a ladle, pour the mulled wine through a small strainer into mugs and garnish each with a cinnamon stick.

Sangria

A party-perfect wine-based punch from Spain to serve with tapas. Feel free to experiment with different combinations of wines and fruits.

Serves 25

4	oranges, scrubbed thoroughly
2	lemons, scrubbed thoroughly
2	limes, scrubbed thoroughly
Two 750-ml	bottles of red wine, traditionally Rioja or another Spanish red
1	cup Orange Brandy or Orange Vodka (page 18)
1/3 to 1	cup superfine sugar
1-liter	bottle of sparkling water or club soda

Chill all the liquid ingredients. Using a vegetable peeler or zester, remove the zest from 1 orange in a continuous spiral, being careful not to include any of the white pith. Place the zest in a 2-quart (2-liter) container. Juice the zested orange, 2 of the remaining oranges, 1 of the lemons, and 1 of the limes, and add to the container. Cut the remaining orange, lemon, and lime into thin slices. Add to the citrus juices along with the wine, brandy, and sugar to taste. Stir to dissolve the sugar. Chill the sangria for 3 to 4 hours. Pour into a punch bowl or pitchers and discard the orange zest. Slowly pour in the sparkling water. Stir gently.

Spiked Mulled Cider

A recipe with roots in medieval times, fragrant and festive mulled cider warms up a cold autumn night.

3   whole nutmegs

1   gallon fresh-pressed nonalcoholic apple cider

1/4 to 1   cup sugar

Zest of one well-scrubbed orange, cut into 1/2-inch-wide strips

Zest of one well-scrubbed lemon, cut into 1/2-inch-wide strips

5   cinnamon sticks, each broken into about 3 pieces

2   tablespoons whole cloves

1   cup Apple Brandy (page 13)

Using a nutcracker, crack the whole nutmegs into pieces. (Or place them in a plastic bag and crack with a mallet.) In a large pot, combine all the ingredients except the brandy. Bring to a boil. Reduce heat to low and simmer for 30 minutes. Remove the cider from the heat and strain into a heat-proof glass bowl. Stir in the brandy. Serve in mugs.

Sparkling Punch

Serves
25

What the movie stars—think Ava Gardner, Cary Grant, and Katharine Hepburn—were drinking on yachts off Catalina Island in the 1940s.

1	cup superfine sugar
1-liter	bottle of sparkling water
One 750-ml	bottle of Burgundy
1	cup Orange Brandy or Orange Vodka (page 18)
	Large block of ice
Two 750-ml	bottles of brut Champagne or sparkling wine
4	oranges, scrubbed thoroughly and cut into slices

Chill all the liquid ingredients. In a small bowl, dissolve the sugar in 1 cup of the sparkling water. Pour into a punch bowl. Add the Burgundy and brandy, then stir. Add the ice, Champagne, and remaining sparkling water. Garnish with the orange slices.

After-Dinner Drinks

Brandy Alexander

Popular in the 1930s (using gin instead of brandy), and attributed to Harry MacElhone of Harry's New York Bar in Paris, the cocktail was first known as the Panama and then as the Alexander Number 2. Despite its rather old-fashioned reputation, it makes a luscious dessert or nightcap.

Serves 1

1 **ounce brandy**

1 **ounce Chocolate Vodka (page 17)**

1 **ounce heavy cream**

1 **cup cracked ice**

Cocoa powder, ground nutmeg, or ground cinnamon

Combine the brandy, vodka, cream, and cracked ice in a shaker. Shake for 10 to 15 seconds, then strain into a chilled old-fashioned glass. Garnish with a sprinkle of cocoa powder.

Black Russian

Serves 1

An infused version of the classic black-velvet cocktail created by barman Gustave Tops of the Hotel Metropole in Brussels in the 1950s. Legend says it was mixed for American ambassador Pearl Mesta.

- 3 1/2 **cups Coffee Vodka, Coffee Rum, or Coffee Brandy (page 19)**
- 1 1/2 **ounces plain vodka or Vanilla Vodka (page 34)**
- 1 **cup cracked ice**

Combine all of the ingredients in a shaker. Shake for 10 to 15 seconds, then strain into a chilled old-fashioned glass.

Café Cocktail

Serves 1

Sophisticated and sweet, but not headache-inducing sugary, the café cocktail was included in *Esquire*'s 1939 "Potables" column.

- 1 **ounce brandy**
- 1 **ounce Chocolate Vodka (page 17)**
- 2 **ounces black coffee**
- 1 **teaspoon superfine sugar, or to taste**
- 1 **cup cracked ice**
- 1 **lemon twist**

Combine the brandy, vodka, coffee, sugar (if desired), and cracked ice in a shaker. Shake for 10 to 15 seconds, then strain into a chilled cocktail glass. Garnish with the lemon twist.

Café Grog

Hot and bracing, the perfect last drink before heading
back out into the cold.

Serves 1

1	ounce Spiced Vodka (page 30)
1/2	ounce plain brandy
2	teaspoons superfine sugar
1/2	cup black coffee or espresso
1	lemon twist

Combine the vodka, brandy, sugar, and coffee in a small
saucepan. Bring to a simmer. Pour into a mug and garnish
with the lemon twist.

Grasshopper

Serves 1

Embrace your secret love of kitsch. The grasshopper was the cliché of 1970s dinner parties, but don't hold a grudge—this is a satiny and decadent drink. Crème de cacao, a chocolate liqueur, may be used in place of the white chocolate–infused vodka.

1   ounce Mint Vodka (page 23)

1   ounce White Chocolate Vodka (page 17), Vanilla Vodka (page 34), or crème de cacao

1   ounce heavy cream

    Drop of green food coloring (optional)

1   cup cracked ice

1   teaspoon white chocolate shavings

Combine the vodkas, cream, food coloring (if desired), and cracked ice in a shaker. Shake for 10 to 15 seconds, then strain into a chilled old-fashioned glass. Garnish with the white chocolate shavings.

Hot Mint Chocolate

Mint Vodka makes hot chocolate taste like Thin Mint cookies.

Serves 1

- **1 quart whole milk**
- **1/2 cup coarsely chopped semisweet chocolate**
- **1 cup Mint Vodka (page 23)**
- **4 peppermint sticks**

In a saucepan over medium heat, warm the milk until it begins to steam, about 5 minutes. Add the chocolate and stir until it melts into the milk. Add the vodka and stir for a few seconds. Divide among 4 mugs and serve each with a peppermint stick garnish.

Hot Buttered Spiced Rum

Serves 1

The fine folks of New England of yore came up with this spicy drink—and it's been a classic ever since. The butter adds a rich smoothness.

2 teaspoons sugar

1/2 cup hot water

2 ounces Spiced Rum (page 30)

1/2 teaspoon unsalted butter

Ground nutmeg

In a mug, dissolve the sugar in a small amount of the hot water. Add the rum and butter. Top off with the remaining hot water and stir. Garnish with a sprinkle of nutmeg.

Mexican Hot Chocolate

Serves 1

Cinnamon-infused vodka lends spice to the sweetness, while an ancho chile adds subtle heat.

1 quart whole milk

1 ancho chile, quartered and seeds removed

1/2 cup coarsely chopped semisweet chocolate

1 cup Cinnamon Vodka (page 30)

Ground cinnamon

In a saucepan over medium heat, combine the milk and ancho chile. Heat until the milk begins to steam, about 5 minutes. Add the chocolate and stir until it melts into the milk. Discard the chile. Add the vodka and stir for a few seconds. Divide among 4 mugs and garnish each with a sprinkle of ground cinnamon.

Milk Punch

Milk punch was imbibed from colonial times through World War II. It fell out of favor, but for no good reason—it's spicy, delicious, and lovely served hot.

Serves 1

> 2 ounces Spiced Rum or Spiced Brandy (page 30)
>
> 1 teaspoon superfine sugar
>
> 1 cup whole milk
>
> 1 cup cracked ice
>
> Ground nutmeg

Combine the rum, sugar, milk, and cracked ice in a shaker. Shake for 10 to 15 seconds, then strain into a chilled old-fashioned glass. Garnish with a sprinkle of nutmeg.

Pumpkin Pie

Spicy-sweet frothy goodness—a great after-dinner drink from Halloween through the New Year.

Serves 1

> 1 ounce Pumpkin Vodka (page 29)
>
> 1 ounce Vanilla Vodka (page 34)
>
> 1 ounce heavy cream
>
> 1 cup cracked ice
>
> Ground cinnamon

Combine the vodkas, cream, and cracked ice in a shaker. Shake for 10 to 15 seconds, then strain into a chilled cocktail glass. Garnish with a sprinkle of cinnamon.

Strawberry Meringue

Creamy, sweet, and voluptuous, this is the Marilyn Monroe of cocktails. Excellent for a hot summer night.

Serves 1

- **2 ounces Vanilla Vodka (page 34)**
- **1 ounce Strawberry Vodka (page 15)**
- **1 ounce heavy cream**
- **2 tablespoons strawberry purée (page 117)**
- **1 cup cracked ice**
- **1 strawberry, cut into slices**

Combine the vodkas, cream, strawberry purée, and cracked ice in a shaker. Shake for 10 to 15 seconds, then strain into a chilled cocktail glass. Garnish with the strawberry slices.

Toasted Almond Milk

So simple and pure that it almost seems wholesome.

Serves 1

- **4 or 5 ice cubes**
- **2 ounces Almond Vodka or Almond Brandy (page 32)**
- **1/2 cup whole milk**
- **1 cup cracked ice**

Place the ice cubes in a chilled old-fashioned glass. Combine the vodka, milk, and cracked ice in a shaker. Shake for 10 to 15 seconds, then strain into the glass.

White Hot Chocolate

Vanilla Vodka and melted white chocolate make for an unexpected variation on an old favorite. Vanilla Rum or Vanilla Brandy may be substituted.

Serves 4

- **1 quart whole milk**
- **1/2 cup coarsely chopped white chocolate**
- **1 cup Vanilla Vodka (page 34)**
- **2 tablespoons white chocolate shavings**

In a saucepan over medium heat, warm the milk until it begins to steam, about 5 minutes. Add the white chocolate and stir until it melts into the milk. Add the vodka and stir for a few seconds.

Divide among 4 mugs and garnish each with white chocolate shavings.

White Russian

The first White Russian dates to the 1920s and was originally made with crème de cacao. Coffee-infused vodka adds a heady intensity of flavor. Coffee Rum or Coffee Brandy may be substituted.

1	ounce Vanilla Vodka (page 34)
1	ounce Coffee Vodka (page 19)
1 to 2	tablespoons heavy cream
1	cup cracked ice

Combine the vodkas, cream, and cracked ice in a shaker. Shake for 10 to 15 seconds, then strain into a chilled old-fashioned glass.

Le Cognac aux Truffe

The Bar Hemingway at the Ritz Paris has perfected the art of infusion—or maceration, as the bartenders there call it. In 2000, Christophe Léger, one of the legendary bartenders, began experimenting with truffles infused in various spirits, finally deciding that Cognac carried the perfume of the truffle the best. The infusion took Paris by storm and is considered the perfect cocktail after a decadent French meal.

Serves 1 very special person

Pour Truffle Liqueur (page 33) in a Bordeaux glass. Enjoy.

Sources for Ingredients

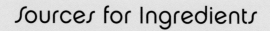

Almost all of the ingredients for making infused liqueurs can be found at a local grocery store, liquor store, or gourmet shop. Here are sources for items that may be a bit harder to find.

BLUEBERRY HONEY	Bee Raw Honey Products, 212-941-1932 beeraw.com
CANDIED FLOWERS	Dean & DeLuca, 877-826-9246 deananddeluca.com
FRUIT-FLAVORED SYRUPS (SUCH AS MANGO)	Barista Pro Shop, 866-776-5288 baristaproshop.com
LAVENDER HONEY	Bainbridge Farms, 800-539-9066 bainbridgefarms.com
NATURAL FOOD COLORING	Nature's Flavors, 714-744-3700 naturesflavors.com
ORGANIC LAVENDER	Dean & DeLuca, 877-826-9246 deananddeluca.com; Sage Kitchen Ltd., 403-933-4882 sagekitchen.com
ORGANIC ROSE PETALS	Mountain Rose Herbs, 800-879-3337 mountainroseherbs.com; Sage Kitchen Ltd., 403-933-4882 sagekitchen.com
ORGANIC VIOLET PETALS	Mountain Rose Herbs, 800-879-3337 mountainroseherbs.com; Sage Kitchen Ltd., 403-933-4882 sagekitchen.com
TRUFFLES	Truffle Market, 800-822-4003 trufflemarket.com
WILD BLUEBERRY SYRUP	Maine Munchies, 866-480-0000 gladstones@mainemunchies.com

Index

Index

Index

Liquid Measurements

Bar spoon	=	$1/2$ ounce
1 teaspoon	=	$1/6$ ounce
1 tablespoon	=	$1/2$ ounce
2 tablespoons (pony)	=	1 ounce
3 tablespoons (jigger)	=	1 $1/2$ ounces
$1/4$ cup	=	2 ounces
$1/3$ cup	=	3 ounces
$1/2$ cup	=	4 ounces
$2/3$ cup	=	5 ounces
$3/4$ cup	=	6 ounces
1 cup	=	8 ounces
1 pint	=	16 ounces
1 quart	=	32 ounces
750-ml bottle	=	25.4 ounces
1-liter bottle	=	33.8 ounces
1 medium lemon	=	3 tablespoons juice
1 medium lime	=	2 tablespoons juice
1 medium orange	=	$1/3$ cup juice